Taking Action
in Organizations
and Communities

Second Edition

John L. Erlich • Jack Rothman • Joseph G. Teresa

eb
eddie bowers publishing co., inc.

Exclusive marketing and distributor rights for U.K., Eire,
and Continental Europe held by:

Gazelle Book Services Limited
Falcon House
Queen Square
Lancaster
LA1 1RN
U.K.

---

eddie bowers publishing co., inc.
P.O. Box 130
Peosta, Iowa 52068-0130 USA

www.eddiebowerspublishing.com

ISBN 0-945483-88-0

Printed in the United States of America.

9 8 7 6 5 4 3

Contents

Preface   v
About the Authors   vi

1   A Systematic Approach to Change   1

Research and Common Sense   5
The Structure of the Manual   7
How to Use the Manual   8
The Right to Decide and Act   10
Conclusion   13
Notes   13

2   Promoting and Innovation   15

Research on Innovation   16
Operationalizing the Guideline   20
Patterns of Implementation   21
Practitioners' Views of Problems and Prospects   31
Getting Started   36
   Initial Log Form   37
   Initial Log: A Preliminary Guide for Action   38
   Illustrations of Initial Logs Completed by Practitioners   47
Notes   48

3   Changing and Organization's Goals   49

Research on Organization's Goals   51
Operationalizing the Guideline   55
Patterns of Implementation   63
Practitioner's Views of Problems and Prospects   67
Getting Started   73
   Initial Log Form   74
   Initial Log: A Preliminary Guide for Action   75
   Illustrations of Initial Logs Completed by Practitioners   84
Notes   85

4 Fostering Participation   87

Research on Participation   89
Illustrating and Operationalizing the Guideline   91
Perspectives from Behavior Modification   98
Patterns of Implementation   101
Practitioners' Views of Problems and Prospects   103
Getting Started   107
    Initial Log Form   110
    Initial Log: A Preliminary Guide for Action   110
    Illustrations of Initial Logs Completed by Practitioners   120
Notes   121

5 Increasing the Effectiveness of Role Performance   123

Guidelines from Research on Role Conflict   124
Operationalizing the Guideline   127
Patterns of Implementation   132
Practitioners' Views of Problems and Prospects   140
Getting Started   144
    Initial Log Form   145
    Initial Log: A Preliminary Guide for Action   145
    Illustrations of Initial Logs Completed by Practitioners   155
Notes   157

6 Conclusion   159

Sequencing of Guidelines   159
Some Final Comments   162
Note   164

Appendix: A Note on the Research Methodology Shaping the Book   165

Preface

We are very pleased to present this revision of a book based on original, ground-breaking research done at the University of Michigan School of Social Work. If anything, the change focus on organizations and communities is more urgent today than when the first printing was published in 1981.

Despite proud rhetoric to the contrary, and often-expressed commitments to broad ecological intervention models and generalist practice designs, the reality of most social work efforts in which both students and social agencies are engaged focus on individuals, families, and small groups. The constraints imposed by recent fundamental changes in "welfare as we know it," have resulted in less, rather than more, broad innovation, challenges to the status quo, and willingness to take much risk on behalf of clients.

Our interest in knowing about your experiences in using these strategies in the "real world" continues. We look forward to hearing from you.

Professor John L. Erlich
Sacramento, California
January, 1998

bout the Authors

JOHN. L. ERLICH is a Professor of Social Work at California State University, Sacramento, where he has been Chairperson of the Child and Family Services Program and the Policy, Planning, and Administration Program. He previously taught at the University of Michigan School of Social Work. Widely published, he has developed training materials for organizers and planners working in a wide range of organizational and community settings, and served as an organizer and program developer in Northern California, Michigan, and New York City.

JACK ROTHMAN is Professor Emeritus at the University of California, Los Angeles, and previously taught at the University of Michigan School of Social Work and the University of Pittsburgh. He also practiced community organization and group work in various social agencies in New York City. Dr. Rothman has conducted research and written widely in the areas of community and organizational change, race and ethnic relations, and the utilization of social science research for designing social interventions.

JOSEPH G. TERESA has worked in the U.S. Department of Education's Office of Management and Evaluation. Previously, he taught at the University of Maryland and the University of Michigan School of Social Work. A distinguished researcher in the human services, Dr. Teresa has published extensively in that field.

1

A Systematic Approach to Change

There are growing frustrations over the failures and limitations of human service programs and projects geared to social change. The titles of two recent books on change are significant: *Why Organizers Fail* and *Community Organization: Studies in Constraint.*[1] Both books provide vivid illustrations of how grass roots organizers and social planners in a wide range of situations are utterly frustrated and defeated in their efforts to accomplish their goals. One of the authors observes: "Community programs directed to significant social change have probably failed more often than they have succeeded. (Social systems) have proven inordinately complex and intractable to planned intervention."[2]

The task of the direct service worker, planner, organizer, or administrator is formidable. Often goals are broad, idealistic, and unpopular (welfare rights, affirmative action, improved mental health). There may be strong organizational or community resistance to innovative approaches or to increased service budgets. Even more opposition may be engendered to programs involving shifts in social status, established ideology, or power relationships. But part of the problem may lie with the practitioner and the tools he or she[3] brings to the job.

This manual is a preliminary effort to confront that issue. The difficulty with "do-gooders" (a mixed category composed variously of human service workers, community volunteers , liberals, radicals, and other socially concerned individuals) is not that their goals are wrong or that they meddle where they should not, but that they do not meddle very well. The fundamental purpose of this book is to provide effective strategies that will enable the "doing of good" in execution as well as in intent.

We have attempted to achieve a meaningful synthesis of theory and practice. Appropriate research findings from the social science literature were retrieved and codified, and generalizations were developed in areas pertinent to community and organizational change, such as participation and diffusion of innovations. These generalizations were then converted into their applied form. The resulting "action guidelines" were field-tested, retested, and re-fined.[4] They are set down in this practice manual in a form that allows them to be widely disseminated and easily replicated. The general method is analogous to the research-development-diffusion model employed in the physical sciences and, particularly, in industry.

In this book we not only offer specific strategies or action guidelines for people who work in human service agencies but also suggest some tactical steps for effectively carrying out these strategies. At the same time, detailed attention is given to *personal, client organizational,* and *community* factors that bear on a practitioner's attempts to achieve a specified objective with a particular strategy. Examples given by practitioners demonstrate the specific ways in which the guidelines were actually carried out in settings that ranged from neighborhood centers to statewide mental health organizations. The organizations and agencies in which the action guidelines were field-tested included such disparate settings as an urban planning council, community mental health center, social welfare workers union, family service agency, a health department, YMCA, urban redevelopment, intermediate school district, juvenile court, and a drug abuse planning council.

This book is an abridged, more practice-oriented revision of a longer volume by the authors entitled *Promoting Innovation and Change in Organizations and Communities: A Planning Manual* (Wiley, 1976). Revisions were based on feedback from practitioners in the field who used the earlier version. In streamlining the original publication, we omitted technical research information an unessential illustrations and generally geared the text to on-the-line agency and community professionals. Further information about the research that shaped the contents of this book can be found in the Appendix and in various publications of the Community Intervention Project.[5]

The subject matter has been called planning, organizational change, community work, diffusion of innovations, service delivery, social action, and the like. Under whatever name, we deal with interventions that are oriented toward influencing social services and institutions and solving community welfare problems. This activity is performed by human service professionals from several disciplines as well as by citizen volunteers in civic associations and political action groups. Most of these activities have multiple but related purposes such as establishing and improving human service programs, directing and coordinating such programs, maintaining community organizations and relationships, modifying or reforming institutions and practices, and conducting programs of community relations and public education.[6]

There is a conception of the social change process that influences the general approach taken in the manual. We assume that change, particularly in the human service fields, takes place in a series of incremental steps. Even revolutionary change must be viewed in terms of sequential tactical actions and reactions, building up to a culminating event that radically transforms a society.

From this point of view, a practitioner should proceed by setting a sequence of goals that are specific, realistic, and *proximate*—that is, short-run and tangible. A general objective is approached by moving through incremental stages; the attainment of one stage leads to the sighting and definition of the goal for the next one.

To employ the manual effectively, then, one must scale down a given purpose to a goal of limited size and time dimensions, so that it can be achieved within approximately 5 to 12 weeks. The setting of such limited goals is crucial to the entire enterprise. The practitioner then can be sure of what he is attempting and can be clear about whether it has been achieved. Both rational strategy and meaningful evaluation grow out of this.

There is a common tendency in the human services to speak of our goals in such grand terms as building a better community, improving social functioning, making institutions more responsive to people, or eliminating poverty or racism. It is sometimes difficult to move from these emotionally satisfying big objectives to ones that are finite and feasible. It may be uncomfortable to shift to "thinking small," but it is also necessary. This kind of specification and delimitation has permitted many of the strategies illustrated in this manual to be achieved in about two or three months.

This approach to goals has the added benefit of permitting greater accountability. When goals are formulated in such global generalizations as "promoting human welfare," it is difficult to be responsible for failure or clear about success. Certainly in some situations, for political and organizational reasons, it is necessary for practitioners to be somewhat vague about their objectives. Our aims are high and our practice environment incredibly complex and unpredictable. Protection, through obscuring intentions, may be necessary. However, for many of us this fuzziness has become a habit rather than a necessary defense against potential detractors. Recognizing this shortcoming, we try to lay out a much more deliberate approach to intervention than may be found in most of the literature on social change. We need to say *specifically* what it is that we are trying to do and to be held responsible when things do not turn out as we hoped. This kind of rigorous goal definition permits what we have always said is elusive: evaluation. And certainly accountability is important in keeping faith with the people we serve. At the same time, as a byproduct, the chances of increased learning and competence are enhanced; if we set more precise goals, we can analyze much more systematically what we have done—our weaknesses and strengths, both conceptual and practical.

RESEARCH AND COMMON SENSE

Four principles of intervention, or action guidelines, are considered in the book:

(1) promoting an innovative service or program, by demonstrating it first with a smaller portion of the target population then expanding to the larger group

(2) changing the goals of an organization, by introducing new groups into the organization who support those goals *or* by increasing the influence of those groups within the organization who support those goals

(3) increasing participation in organizations and groups, by offering benefits associated with participation

(4) increasing effectiveness in role performance, by clarifying the role and obtaining agreement about it among relevant superiors and influentials.

Now, it is clear that these principles do not state startling, unusually sophisticated, or esoteric ideas. In our view, these strategies are basic to social intervention.

Research has demonstrated that many commonly accepted and widely used approaches are wrong. Urban renewal programs, instead of aiding intended beneficiaries, increase misery; approaches to juvenile delinquency prevention falter and fail; mental health practices are found to be wanting; and the selection of clients penalizes the people most in need of service. Planners muddle community programs by inappropriate types of coordination or misguided approaches to involvement of participants.

When research supports a given initiative, this is a genuine "finding"—because the opposite result was just as likely. When systematic research *and* practice common sense jointly sustain a strategy or technique, as they do with these guidelines, this is strong authentication that should not be taken lightly.

While the listed guidelines have been derived from social science research, and field experience with them in operating agencies has given the authors confidence in their utility, they are not presented as a panacea or a routing prescription. The particular strategy or action principle embodied in the guideline is not the only or even the best option for attaining the given goal in a particular practice situation. Thus we offer here an *available* strategy, not necessarily an optimal strategy, chosen from a range of alternatives.

The reader will have to rely on his judgment in the application: Does this initiative fit my practice situation? Am I comfortable with it organizationally or ideologically? Does it seem as good as or better than alternative approaches that come to mind?

The effort to tighten up practice has ramifications. Opportunities for practitioners have been reduced since the "golden era" of social programs (the early and middle 1960s). It is all too tempting to orient our concerns toward the arenas to which the money seems to be going. In our judgment, this is shortsighted. The rapid expansion of the human services field in the 1960s did not allow for the serious and systematic attention to the components of social intervention that could have led to further systematic development;

indeed, there were very few attempts to get at the "basics" of intervention. We went with the fads and the fashions, and now we are paying the price: We are blamed for the failures of programs designed by others primarily for cosmetic purposes. It is high time to rebuild from a more solid base of knowledge. Common and uncommon sense, both practice wisdom and research findings, are necessary for that task.

THE STRUCTURE OF THE MANUAL

Each of the next four chapters presents and analyzes one of the four action guidelines described earlier. A final chapter will draw some conclusions and suggest further steps, including ways of sequencing use of the different guidelines.

The general format of the four guideline chapters is similar:

(1) introduction to the practice problem

(2) action principles derived from research on the problem

(3) illustrations of implementation — patterns and operations

(4) practitioners' view of problems and prospects

(5) getting started: thoughts for initiating action and an initial log for listing first steps.

Slight variations will be made in several chapters because specifics in the subject matter suggest different emphases in the presentation.

In the short introductory section we consider why this problem is important, how it affects practitioners, their organizations, and their clients, and various other dimensions of the problem.

The next section cites and briefly reviews important research on the problem and makes a generalization from this research. The principle or action guideline derived from the generalization is then stated, and its important conceptual, definitional, and practical aspects are described.

We next illustrate the action principle as it was actually carried out. A number of different patterns of implementation are given when variations were found. These indicate specific steps and stages the practitioners followed in executing the guideline. We also indicate how each of the elements of the guidelines was operationalized. (Operationalization pertains to the way *concepts* in the action guideline statement are converted into *real world actions, provisions, materials,* and so on.)

Next, practitioners speak of their experiences in their own words: techniques tried, resistances, confusions, successes, as well as advice they would give to others about how to maneuver.

Each chapter concludes with a section on *Getting Started*. Here questions are asked to help the practitioner through the thinking process needed to initiate action with the guideline. This is followed by a *Guide to Action* initial log form on which preliminary reflections about beginning action steps can be set down. Here the emphasis is on specifying a goal that is proximate—moderate in size and concrete. (Again we feel obligated to underscore the importance of this step.) The initial log also calls for preliminary thoughts about how each of the elements of the guideline might be operationalized, as well as about which key groups and individuals might be involved. Examples from the field experience are given in order to aid in filling out the form.

HOW TO USE THE MANUAL

Different readers will use the manual in different ways. It is possible to start from one's practice situation and then look through the manual to see if any of the guidelines fit. The other way is to start with a guideline that is of interest and then to search one's practice situation for an appropriate problem to which to apply it. It will not be difficult to find a match between practice and the guidelines. The order of presentation of guidelines in the book is somewhat arbitrary. Users should not feel limited to this sequence in their study or application.

After reading the contents of a chapter, filling out the initial log in the Guide to Action is the crucial mobilizing step. To reiterate, *selecting a well-defined and short-term goal is of the highest importance.* A word of warning: The action principles look very simple, but this is deceptive; their implementation is very complex and demands patience and perseverance. The requirements for integration of concepts and actions, and for clarity and specification in designing strategy, are alien to most practice behavior in this field.

Although the initial log form is short and placed toward the end of a given chapter, its size and location should not obscure its saliency in using this manual. A proportionately much longer period of time should be anticipated for working with the initial log than for reading and digesting the concepts and data in the chapter itself.

In our use of the manual we have found it helpful initially for people to work in teams of two to four members. In this way they may collaborate in developing the initial log, applying it to a practice situation that one or two of them experience. Therefore, not every user needs to have a pertinent practice circumstance immediately available; those available may be shared. Groups have found it of interest to summarize their deliberations on newsprint and place these on the wall for others to see.

While this book is termed a practice manual, by now it should be clear that it is not analogous to a technical blueprint. It offers a general strategic direction (such as partializing or providing benefits) to achieve a specific desired practice objective (such as promoting an innovation or fostering participation). Some typical steps or possible alternative steps are suggested, as well as factors to consider in planning, and obstacles that may be anticipated. One cannot expect to proceed step by step in cookbook fashion. The user's intelligence, sensitivity, judgment, creativity, and moral choice are essential, and are in no way mitigated by the relevant social science knowledge that is offered to facilitate implementation.

Use of these guidelines and the procedures associated with them has two additional benefits. First, the approach encourages more self-conscious, deliberate planning in promoting social change. It also offers a useful tool for diagnosing a practice situation and developing a systematic problemsolving style. Second, use of a guideline forces one's professional attention to be focused on a problem.

THE RIGHT TO DECIDE AND ACT

This book is written to provide knowledge that will enhance the competence of people concerned with human betterment by assisting them to become more precise and effective in attaining their goals. It is assumed that professional change agents do indeed seek to produce specific ends and that they hold the responsibility and should enhance their capability to achieve such ends. These goals are of course mediated through the interplay of various constituencies and interested parties such as clients, board members, organizational supervisors, and political elites. Frequently the community practitioner sees her fundamental role as facilitating the decision-making capacity of these relevant actors. Nevertheless, as Morris[7] has suggested, "the exercise of professional leadership requires us to select our goals for action . . . our concern with helping others to make up their minds does not excuse us from the obligation of making up our own."

Many practitioners in the human service fields cripple their effectiveness through a muddy engagement with terms such as "self-determination," "participatory democracy," and "manipulation."

This does not imply that such concepts are unimportant or meaningless. But their application is highly complex, and not particularly aided by philosophical sloganeering. In making a study of the self-determination notion, one observer points out several contingencies that shape its applicability: clients may be ambivalent or contradictory concerning their true desires; reality factors such as legal restrictions, conditions of health, or financial insufficiencies may limit certain wishes; one person's desires may impinge on the prerogatives of others, and may even destroy the people closest to him or oppress those further away. Human worth, the author concludes, is of greater utility as a concept in giving value direction to professional behavior. "If what the client wants will result in the exploitation of others or the degradation of himself, the worker should try to help him change his desires."[8]

Studies of social processes have found that broad public attention and participation may have deleterious effects on such social goals as desegregation of school systems, fluoridation of drinking water, and the passage of millage proposals to improve public education. A change agent seeking to promote such goals would do well to ponder relative values and social benefits attached to generating a great deal of public awareness and activity or proceeding in a more private manner. The well-known political tactic of keeping the situation "quiet" while getting your own supporters out is not to be dismissed lightly.

Contrary to much rhetorical posturing, "enabling" or "participation" is not the method of choice in all situations. If a change agent is to be only a docile, automatic expeditor of whatever decisions are made by others, then human service professional schools are greatly overtraining their students. If the practitioner does not stand ready to thwart wishes that promote racism, hatred, or exploitation, his function is tarnished.

While there are limits on the self-determination concept, there are also constraints on professional intervention. We do not imply that a practitioner needs to be assertive in all activities; although that is certainly an option, and on occasion, a requirement. Surely, while oriented toward particular social objectives, the practitioner needs to be guided also by the outlook and wishes of others, to be highly sensitive regarding when to hold back or to defer to other affected or interested publics. Cheating, lying, bullying, and brutalizing are all incompatible with human values. Enhancing the opportunity for choice is an objective that should be optimized whenever feasible; and if the practitioner's reasoned intention is to increase participation, research-based strategies to support that aim will be found in this volume.

The strategies offered are meant to be used by practitioners in planning their work. But other people may also be consulted and involved in determining if and how to apply the guidelines. Groups of citizens or community professionals can use the guidelines themselves directly in analyzing a problem, or the practitioner may make the information or approach available to various community and agency groups as a resource to them to guide their deliberations.

Important as they are, such value questions are not given prominence in this volume; the function of the book is to make change agents more knowledgeable from a "scientific" standpoint. This should enable them to better *manipulate* their relevant world. That evocative term is deliberately used because, frowned upon as it is, *manipulation* is the business of the professional—acting on or changing the social or physical environment in some valued direction (architects aim to create more beautiful or functional buildings; doctors to improve health; and teachers to develop better informed citizens). Being calculating in goal-oriented activity needs to be distinguished from engaging in dishonest, illegal, arrogant, or despotic behavior.

In some of the human service fields, in particular social work, value considerations have dominated discourse in a disproportionate way. This book aims to counterbalance such valid concern by shifting attention to such equally critical matters as competence, incisiveness, accountability, and predictability in performance.

We cannot offer a formula for resolving the complex ethical and moral issues involved in taking responsibility for social outcomes. The reader will have to make assessments along these lines in reviewing and appraising the various illustrations of practice found throughout the manual.

CONCLUSION

No manual in this field could possibly cover all of the contingencies and ambiguities of practice, even in the mobilization of the simplest strategies. There is not now, nor in all probability will there ever be, an "ultimate" guide to social intervention or politics. But practice can be made less mysterious, less conceived in vague generalizations, and less clothed in an aura of an art that you either "have or have not got." We are prepared to be called to account for what is contained in this volume. Theory has been put to the acid test in the application and operationalized to a considerable extent. Either it can be made to work in the turbulent cross-currents that are always part of practice or we will have failed. Our experience with more than 600 practitioners over a period of fifteen years suggests that the material can indeed be used and that it can bring about successful outcomes. Not inevitably, but if the guidelines are applied with care, and if the limiting conditions are taken into account, a reasonable, acceptable degree of success may be anticipated in the pursuit of humanistic ends.[9]

Notes

1. Harry Brill, *Why Organizers Fail: The Story of a Rent Strike* (Berkeley: University of California Press, 1971); Irving A. Spergel, ed., *Community Organization: Studies in Constraint* (Beverly Hills, CA: Sage Publications, 1972).
2. Spergel, *op. cit.,* p. 9.

3. In the interest of brevity, future references will be to the generic "he."
4. "Field testing" implies examining the feasibility and specifications of a new method or product, not statistically validating a hypothesis.
5. Jack Rothman, Joseph G. Teresa, and John L. Erlich, *Developing Effective Strategies of Social Intervention: A Research and Development Methodology*, PB 272454 TR-1-RD, National Technical Information Service, Springfield, VA 1977; Jack Rothman, *Social R&D: Research and Development in the Human Services* (Englewood Cliffs, NJ: Prentice-Hall, 1980)
6. We have been guided by the conceptual orientation to social intervention in Jack Rothman, "Three Models of Community Organization Practice," *Strategies of Community Organization,* Third Edition, Fred Cox, John L. Erlich, Jack Rothman, and John E. Tropman (Itasca, IL: F.E. Peacock, 1979)
7. Robert Morris, "Community Planning for Health— The Social Welfare Experience," in Public Health Concepts in Social Work Education (New York: Council on Social Work Education, 1961), pp. 168-169.
8. Saul Bernstein, "Self-Determination: King or Citizen in the Realm of Values?," *Social Work, 5*, (1) (January 1960), 3-8.
9. Also see Bruce Jannson, "Why has the American Welfare State been Reluctant?" in *The Reluctant Welfare State* (3rd Ed), (Pacific Grove: CA: Brooks/Cole, 1997), pp. 347–371.

2

Promoting an Innovation

The human service professions have often been characterized as change-oriented. For this reason the process of the diffusion and adoption of innovations invites our attention. Practitioners are constantly involved in promoting new programs, new techniques, new tactics, and new ideas that they wish to propagate in working with target and client systems of various kinds. In many cases these new programs are already well-established elsewhere and are only "new" in terms of being transposed to that particular situation. On the other hand the innovation is sometimes an entirely unique creation of the practitioner and the people he is associated with (for example, the "sit-in" as a tactic or an initial shelter for battered women as a program). In either case, the process followed in promoting the idea and the problems to be encountered is apt to be similar.

Often a practitioner is overwhelmed or immobilized in introducing an innovation because the task seems so large, the obstacles so disarming, and the time available so restrictive. One practitioner discussed her situation in the following terms:

> I had been working on an individual basis with a number of pregnant girls who attended programs at our community center. Because of this activity I was asked to serve on the advisory

committee of the board of education School-Age Parent Program. It became obvious to me that the girls were having a very limited educational experience. I saw the need to help them think through what they intended to do and what alternatives were available to them. Many seem to have given up on the idea of any kind of future after high school. Not only would they need help in planning for themselves, but they would need special skills that would help them proceed with their intentions.

After analyzing all this, I became convinced a more substantial guidance program was necessary for them. However, taking into account the usual kinds of attitudes that prevail in the public schools I knew that I would be facing a lot of resistance to an intensive high quality service. Because of all the time I knew would be involved in trying to set up such a program—while still performing all my other duties—I merely thought about this from time to time but took no specific steps.

RESEARCH ON INNOVATION

Fortunately, a fairly comprehensive and systematic literature exists on the subject of diffusion of innovations. Much of the early research was conducted by rural sociologists interested in agricultural extension problems—how new farming methods and materials came to be adopted by farmers. Other fields that have contributed to this area include anthropology, medical sociology, education, and industry. The planned parenthood and public health areas have also stimulated a great deal of interest in recent years.

From a number of these studies by different disciplines and professions we have drawn the following generalization:

Innovations that are amenable to trial on a partial basis will have a higher adoption rate than innovations that necessitate total adoption without an anticipatory trial.[1]

Generally, an innovation is any program, technique, or activity perceived as new by a population group or organization. An innovation, as the term is most often used in the research literature, refers to new technical, professional, and commercial ideas and practices, such as contraceptive devices, new medical equipment, and farming techniques. These are typically legitimate, conventional, and within the normative consensus of a community and its elites. The promotion of broad and radical political change is not usually defined in the diffusion literature, though it seems likely that some applications can be made to this area.

This concept of partialization can be applied in two ways, for which Everett Rogers uses the terms *observability* and *trialability*. That is, an innovation is more likely to be adopted by an individual or group if there is an opportunity, first, to see the innovation in action and witness its results ("observability") or, second, to employ a portion of an innovation before having to employ the total innovation ("trialability"). In observability one typically divides the target population; in trialability one divides the innovation itself. Both approaches may be combined in a given episode. Studies also emphasize the importance of "opinion leadership".

The likelihood that an innovation will be adopted by a larger population is increased if the innovation is first utilized by a smaller group of opinion leaders. This smaller initiating group may be characterized as style setters, information disseminators, key communicators, sparkplugs, or gatekeepers, among other descriptions. Thus innovations frequently take place in a two-step sequence, from a small subsystem of early adopters and opinion leaders to adoption by a larger population or system. The subsystem may use only part of the innovation at the outset.

A useful illustration of these findings is provided by Carlson's study of how the new math became part of the curriculum of schools in Allegheny County, Pennsylvania.[2] Five superintendents who were closely associated with one another introduced the new approach in

1959. As a result of their example and their contacts with other superintendents, an additional 10 schools adopted it in 1960. Then 12 more schools tried it in 1961. By the end of 1963, 38 schools were employing this altogether different method of teaching mathematics. This is a good example of the sequential, snowballing pattern that is found in the dissemination of many innovations.

From this concept of partialization found in the research, we have derived the following action guideline.

> Practitioners wishing to promote an innovation in a general target system should develop it initially in a partial segment of that target system.

Although the generalization permits partializing either the target population or the innovation, for purposes of systematic and consistent treatment the guideline focuses on the target population. A target system is defined as a particular group, organization, community, or society toward which an innovation is directed. In the context of our guideline we are dealing largely with the organizational and subcommunity level. Adoption of the guideline implies an incremental, stepping stone process; success on a small scale with a limited group is used as the basis for promoting a new idea, or having it spread spontaneously, across a wider population. There are many familiar analogues: the demonstration project, the pilot program, the modeling of new roles or behavior, and the free sample. In their book on innovations in organizations, Zaltman and his associates support this action principle: "The more obvious the innovation is, the more likely it is to be adopted. This suggests still another factor. The more amenable to *demonstration* the innovation is, the more visible its advantages are, and thus the more likely it is to be adopted."[3]

Rogers's writings contain concepts from which we can infer some attributes of a partial target system that are conducive to communication and linkage. Communication appears to be facilitated when two groups possess similar outlooks, values, social status, or education. There is more comfort and trust when people are similar; messages are more likely to be sent and received accurately. For some types of situations, then, similarity of the partial and general target systems may be advisable.

On the other hand, Rogers notes that this similarity may also serve as a barrier to communication. New ideas usually enter a system by way of higher status, more cosmopolitan opinion leaders. Characteristics of opinion leaders as determined in mass communications and diffusion studies include higher social status, more education, greater media exposure, more contact with the change agent, and more openness to innovative ideas. Typically, opinion leaders have slightly more of these traits than other individuals at the same social level. These characteristics suggest attributes to be sought in selecting target populations for some types of innovations, particularly those using mass communications as the medium of transmittal.

As we noted earlier, radical ideas, or a context of intense political conflict, would not provide a suitable setting for this guideline. The strategy is most useful when the innovation is reasonable legitimate and conventional, and when the following conditions are present:

(1) The cost of large-scale application is high while the cost of a limited demonstration is small.

(2) There is little or no information about the value or cost of a large-scale application.

(3) The process is not easily reversible once it is begun.

(4) A large-scale application might alert and mobilize opposition, but a small-scale one would not.

(5) The larger system has little or no receptivity to the innovation.

This incremental, partialization notion can be connected with the idea of *proximate* goals. These are moderate, tangible objectives that can be attained in the short term. Looking at the new math illustration, a partial target system of five superintendents initiated the innovation. A proximate general target system of 10 additional schools had accepted this method in the next year. A practitioner who was attempting ultimately to reach the 38 schools that adopted the innovation (as a general target system) would have performed in a reasoned way by starting out with the 5 + 10 formulation as a lead-in to implementing the guideline. This 15 now constitutes a new *aggregate* partial target group that can be used as the basis for impacting the next stage proximate general target system. One can visualize a rippling effect resulting from casting a pebble into the water. A given proximate general target system is intermediate to where the pebble lands (partial target system) and the farthest out ripple (general target system). The implementation of this guideline, then, may usefully be conceptualized as a series of *incremental stages*.

OPERATIONALIZING THE GUIDELINE

The selection of an appropriate, facilitative partial target system is crucial in carrying out the guideline. That is, the partial system chosen should enhance the probability of the innovation's success on a limited scale. An organizer in a welfare workers union, for example, wanted to introduce a system of implementing the union's programs at the individual building level. He took into account many factors in selecting an initial target building.

> The basic consideration for the successful application of this guideline, at least in my case, was the selection of the target sub-population. I was able to employ the following factors: geographic location, history of organizational activity leading to

cohesiveness (how long had the folks been relating to each other organizationally), leadership (both actual and potential) within the partial target population, level of skill, and experience within the target population.

Figure 2.1 (page 22) illustrates other instances of innovation promotion in order to show the range of innovations to which this guideline has been applied, as well as to demonstrate how other practitioners have applied the concepts of a general target system and partial target system. The chart also indicates the mechanisms by which the transfer was made from the smaller to the larger target system.

PATTERNS OF IMPLEMENTATION

There are two important variations in the patterns of implementation of the guideline. In the first pattern, which we call a "spontaneous" contagion model, the action proceeds from the practitioner (P) to the partial target system to the general target system. This pattern is typical of the agricultural extension approach in which one farmer uses a new seed and is successful; his neighbors see the results and then plant the same seed. It can be depicted as follows:

"Spontaneous" Contagion Model

P → Partial Target System → General Target System

In the second pattern, the action moves from the practitioner to the partial target system, and then to a relevant decision-making unit and from there to the general target system. In other words, a decision-making unit intrudes as a necessary pass-through point between the partial and general target systems. This process typically is used in organizational situations.

Setting	Innovation	General Target	Proximate (short run) Target	Partial Target	Transfer Mechanism
A community mental health center in a semi-rural county.	Stimulate local unions to accept the function of community care givers for their members.	All 200 local unions in the county.	Fifty unions from around the county.	A limited number of union members and leaders participated in a workshop on community care giving—including ten unions	The country-wide (all inclusive) AFL-CIO Labor Educational Committee voted sponsorship of a follow-up workshop to be offered to all county locals.
Traditional settlement house serving a largely black population.	Introducing an intensive educational focus into a program that had been essentially recreational.	Entire school age membership of the settlement house.	The same as general target.	A group of 20 teen members were involved in two educational counseling sessions.	Board of Directors voted an allocation for hiring an educational director to serve the membership.
A regional planning council serving several counties.	Have the planning council gain responsibility for advising HUD on housing applications from all regional municipalities.	All 30 municipalities in the region.	12 municipalities with whom practitioners have had positive previous contact.	With HUD approval, reviewed and assessed trial applications from four municipalities.	HUD approved review procedure for all municipality applications.
A social welfare employees union in a metropolitan community.	Decentralize program implementation through building level unit committees.	All 25 building level units in the union: the total membership.	Six units in a contiguous area.	Shop stewards at a single building location were involved successfully in union program implementation functions.	The union executive board instituted a policy of building level program implementation.

Figure 2.1: Elements of the Innovation Guideline Operationalized

Decision-Making Unit Model

$$\text{Decision-}$$
$$P \to \text{Partial Target System} \to \text{Making} \to \text{General Target System}$$
$$\text{Unit}$$

In the spontaneous contagion process the general target system accepts the innovation directly. In the decision-making unit arrangement a transfer mechanism or agent authorizes the carryover from the smaller to the larger group. The authorization may involve carrying out the program either with or without the prior explicit acceptance of the general target system

Variations on the pattern of practitioner → Partial Target → Decision-Making Unit → General Target are many. Sometimes the practitioner needs initial approval from a supervisor or the agency director. Occasionally he first receives approval from the Decision-Making Unit to carry out the demonstrations, completes it, and returns to the Decision Making Unit for authorization to spread to the general target. In some instances there are two Decision-Making Units involved. Some practitioners arrange to have the Decision-Making Unit experience the demonstration directly as, for example, attending a conference at which a new technique or medium is employed.

Planners and organizers follow both of the basic patterns. An illustration of the spontaneous contagion model is taken from the experience of a president of a social workers union who wished to institute a training program for his executive board, using a method by which case examples and sharing personal experiences are used to enhance effectiveness in dealing with grievance problems. He obtained approval from the board before he began the process.

> I then contacted a select group of four board members, requesting them to participate on the committee. I asked them to present a case example for the meeting and scheduled a committee time with them.

I chaired the committee meeting, suggested the rationale for the model to be used, and assumed responsibility for following up on specific tasks. The committee decided to conduct the training session in front of the board following the format of the committee meeting. Individual contacts were made to publicize the training session. The model was used at the training session, and the response was most favorable as the board had directly seen and experienced what I was trying to get across.

The general target system, the executive board, participated with interest in the training session with positive evaluative comments ("we were really able to share problems in a new way"; "it was really helpful to know that other people had some of the same problems"; and so on).

The key suggestion—at the training session—was that a next target system, for the future, could be the general membership with the same model being applied.

The decision-making unit pattern was followed by a worker in a traditional family service agency who was attempting to develop the concept of outreach services. She believed the agency should work directly with clients in a low-income housing project, rather than expecting them—or, more likely, middle-class substitutes—to come to the agency offices. The problem was to convince the agency board to provide this type of service and the housing manager to clear the way for it to operate within the project.

My use of the guideline involved a small group of residents living on a court in a low-cost housing project. We were able to convince the Housing Authority that social work intervention could make a difference in the social problems in the housing project; reduce the social causes for eviction. A sub-goal was the introduction and sustaining of an outreach program by our agency to housing project residents. We selected one court (5 families) out of the entire project as a demonstration; set up a time limit for evaluative purposes; promised progress reports at specific intervals; and met with the residents regularly as well as just "dropping in." This plan was submitted in writing to the board along with my periodic progress reports.

The plan worked almost too well in that it was constantly referred to in agency Board meetings; the outreach idea was new here; it really impressed the Board and the Housing Director, and was accepted as a legitimate and appropriate agency program. The results with the residents were not as spectacular, but represented at least a beginning, and we gradually expanded to other courts.

In the great majority of cases in our study a formal decision-making unit was necessary to foster or legitimize the transfer and broadening of the innovation.

Another aspect of implementation concerns the amount of effort expended by the practitioner in diffusing the innovation from the partial to the general targets. In some instances the practitioner was very active in promoting the diffusion. For example, the community center worker quoted earlier demonstrated an intensive guidance program for unwed mothers in one high school. She then set out to have the same format introduced throughout the school system:

> I now had to involve additional individuals and groups. I proceeded to develop a proposal and arrange for meetings with the following: my Center's Board of Directors, School Age Parents Advisory Board, Episcopal officials (for funds), school administrators, teachers and students. After a number of meetings and a month and a half, we were able to gain administrative approval and a verbal commitment for funding of the program so all relevant students might benefit.

In other instances, such as with the social work union training program, the partial group did the "selling."

These patterns are identified as a spontaneous process on the one hand and a directed process on the other. In the spontaneous process, the practitioner is active in securing the adoption of the innovation by the partial target, but leaves the diffusion of the innovation to the general target in the hands of the partial target. The diffusion is thus carried out by the partial target, either by active promotion or by "inactive" modeling or example.

By contrast, the directed process involves the practitioner both in the adoption phase of the partial target and in the diffusion phase to the general target system. It may involve the practitioner's "supervision" or encouragement of the partial target system in the diffusion to the general target system, or it may involve the practitioner as the sole "line of communication" between the partial and general target system. Viewed another way, it may be the act of a skeptical practitioner, doubting the validity of the guideline, or it may be the act of a practitioner who recognizes a lack of exact correspondence between the practice problem and the population on which the research was based.

The innovations being promoted by the practitioners fell into two categories. First, some of the practitioners had a fairly concrete detailed "product" to promote—a policy or program for adoption:

(1) to develop a policy statement calling for an increase in the number of psychiatric beds for children in the metropolitan area

(2) to establish the Poverty and Social Problems Curriculum in six schools in the tricounty area

(3) to create a rotating toy library for use by six child care facilities.

Second, some practitioners had a more fluid "process" of participation or involvement as an innovation to be promoted:

(1) a subcommittee or task force of the eight private agencies in Wayne and Oakland Counties involved in institutional work with children to work cooperatively with three representatives of the public sector

(2) small groups of black and white students who will meet together in one junior high school.

There were also differences in the practitioner's attitudes toward the innovation. Some practitioners were convinced of the
validity of the new program. Others, however, were less certain and
saw the guideline as a basis for "testing" rather than "selling." We
have seen the first attitude expressed in several of the previous
examples. In this illustration, a mental health worker describes what
can be considered a feasibility study:

> My first experience involved a program designed for mentally
> retarded adults to prove that such services could be delivered
> with volunteer help, and that response from volunteers would be
> forthcoming. Up until that time the agency had resisted using
> volunteers to any extent. Two small groups of adults were se-
> lected initially by using some Department of Social Services
> community care homes and their residents. Eventually we had
> other home operators asking that their residents be allowed to
> participate, and ultimately we used our experiences in this pro-
> gram to write a proposal to the public school's Adult Education
> Department for a weekly socialization program for 200 mentally
> retarded adults. All of this took planning in great detail initially
> because we could not afford for those first few programs to fail.
>
> We recruited and trained volunteers; we selected the initial
> group with some care; and tried to monitor everything constantly.
>
> Through demonstrating with a small portion of the target
> population, we could then open up the program to the larger target
> population—which we did. If we had not limited the group
> initially we would have had disaster, because we did not have the
> volunteers, the space, the equipment nor the "know how" to
> handle a large group. In addition we did not have the acceptance
> of the agency that this was a viable way to proceed in this
> program.

In the discussion thus far we have spoken of dichotomous categories—for example, a decision-making unit or the lack of one,
spontaneous or directed diffusion—but the processes of social
change are more complex. If we trace the steps of a practitioner in

action, we may correct any tendency to over-simplify. Here the director of a mental health association lists the steps he followed in getting the county mental health board (the general target) to endorse a policy statement calling for the provision of more psychiatric beds for emotionally disturbed children (the partial target was the Children and Youth Committee of the board):

(1) collect basic data identifying the scope of the problem

(2) renew active support of my own organization by presenting the problem to the Board of Directors at its December 2 meeting

(3) discuss the problem informally with Mental Health Act staff

(4) discuss the problem informally with selected members of the Children and Youth Committee

(5) present the issue formally to the Children and Youth Committee

(6) discuss the problem informally with representatives of the State Department of Mental Health

(7) encourage suggestions to meet the problem from members of the Children and Youth Committee and from Mental Health Act and State Department staff

(8) encourage site visits to prospective facilities

(9) elicit a formal recommendation from the Children and Youth Committee to the Full Mental Health Act Board

(10) move to secure support of the full Mental Health Act Board.

Excerpts from his final report convey some of the flavor of this activity:

> I first discussed the need for additional beds informally with several Committee members and with the Committee staff person. These contacts were with people whom I did not feel were resistive on doctrinaire grounds. These people encouraged me to bring the issue to the Committee for general discussion
>
> During the following two weeks, I again talked informally with several Committee members, and also spent some time meeting personally with mental health board staff in an effort to help them understand the nature of the need and the more desirable options available. The key staff person agreed that it would be helpful for me to present basic information to the Committee at its next meeting, and informed the Committee Chairman that I was going to prepare some helpful information.
>
> With staff assistance from my own agency, I researched some of the issues related to inpatient care. . . . It was possible to prepare materials that provided valid answers. . . .
>
> Prior to the actual Committee meeting, I again discussed the matter informally with several Committee members. I discussed the data I was collecting and asked them for their thoughts and suggestions.
>
> At the December 15 meeting I presented the information that had been collected. Surprisingly (to me) there was general agreement about the validity of the data, and little support for the notion that there were alternatives to hospital care for the children in question. Inasmuch as the time seemed right to suggest a formal policy statement, I did so. After some discussion, the policy statement was adopted.
>
> The Committee, through its chairman (a member of the full Board) made its recommendation to the Mental Health Board at its late December meeting. The Board adopted the policy statement and directed the Committee to work for its implementation.

Certain general tentative practice advice may be inferred from information gathered from field experience. First, there are several ways in which you may use personal resources. For example, (1) develop and rely upon good relationships within the agency; (2) select a program to which you are committed and which is logically related to your position or role in the agency; and (3) take advantage of your prior experiences in a deliberate way—select a program and setting in which your experience will be an asset.

In addition, you should consider fostering support for the program at all levels within the agency, particularly at upper levels of the agency. If the program is consistent with your other assignments and tasks in the organization, this can serve to legitimize the activity and allow a concentration of energy as well as an interpenetration of contacts, resources, and other factors.

Both community and client factors may be of assistance. Community participation and community support of your organization and yourself may be significant—build such support or select groups to work with in which such support already exists. Client participation may be important. Their interest in and receptivity to the program or organization are also considerations. Select a program in which clients are interested or work hard to develop such interest.

You are likely to experience limiting forces most intensely within your own agency situation. Such agency limitations frequently result from lack of clarity or instability, so that the clarification of goals, programs, and assignments may be a useful tactic. Since internal lack of funds or staff may be a problem, it would be advisable to plan a program realistically within the means of the agency or think of tapping available external resources. To a lesser extent, the agency's structure may be hindering, or its lack of power or authority may be limiting. Both of these factors suggest strategic considerations in the choice of a program.

The need to manage time and energy efficiently was emphasized by the frequent mention of lack of time and overinvolvement as major personal limitations. Within the client population and the larger community, the biggest limitations are likely to be competition from other activities and lack of knowledge. This calls attention to the educational functions of the practitioner's job (interpretation, communication, public relations) and the need to formulate programs that are meaningful and interesting enough to compete with the many other forces that demand the attention of clients and community people. Like many prescriptions, the materials above should be labelled, *Caution, Use with Care.* They are tentative and suggestive. Your own good judgment should influence your evaluation and use of them.

PRACTITIONERS' VIEWS OF PROBLEMS AND PROSPECTS

General support for the principle underlying the guideline was expressed by a number of practitioners. As one of them noted:

> There is a universality about the application of the principle of spreading innovation from a small group of "converts" to a wider clientele. The key to it is the "experiencing" of the innovation by the small group. The guideline works because it reflects truth about the way people learn anything.

Several practitioners commented that the guideline helped them to be more systematic in their work, for example:

> The guideline serves the purpose of breaking down in concrete terms a specific method for initiating and implementing change. I think it is useful to be specific, purposeful, and sequential in pursuing a goal. This guideline suggests such an orientation.
>
> Given some clarity as to support for its use, the guideline is sensible, practical, doable, and realistic.

Other practitioners noted that it is useful for long (and medium) range planning because operational problems can be seen on a small scale before the innovation is attempted on a large scale. They also felt that the initial experience by a limited portion of the target system was helpful in determining the potential success or failure of the innovation itself.

> You do have an opportunity to work out problems of the innovation and to test its value before trying it on the total target system.
> It allows for a test of the idea or change for the practitioner as well as a strategy for gaining acceptance.

While the practitioners expressed enthusiasm for the ideas behind this mode of action, they also pointed out a wide range of problems related to its execution.

One, the perennial problem of time was noted as was the related factor of the need to select a feasible, moderate-sized proximate goal.

> I guess it was having to be patient before things started happening. Assessment had to constantly take place along with the incredible amount of public relations. At first the pay off is small but it makes the professional more credible.
> The guideline is still valid but there has to be a caution of thinking small and clearly—and limiting the goal sufficiently.
> I would not advise one person to try to work in as many communities as I have attempted to do. It's too much of a workload if responsibilities are not delegated to other leaders and organizations.

Two, the selection of the partial target system was described as both a very important and a difficult task.

> The most difficult thing is defining the appropriate "limited portion" of the target population.

It is important to choose a partial target system that will carry the innovation out with the total target.

I found the most problematic aspect to be getting the larger community involved in the effort.

The experience of a health planner who attempted to establish a preventive patient education program by working first with part of the agency staff illustrates some hazards involved in selecting the partial group.

In some ways, the partialization of staff "backfired" in this situation. In that there was little experience of staff being involved in planning and carrying out such a piece of agency work, those involved became extremely ego-involved and those not directly involved developed a real we-they attitude as though they had no role whatsoever, even though they were needed to help carry out contacts. Apparently in this particular situation, this type of partialization in relation to this particular staff grouping did not work, given the previous experience, attitudes, and total situation.

Another practitioner, a particularly sophisticated and skilled professional, experienced success even in a political and controversial setting, because he had successfully chosen the partial target:

I believe that the guideline's use produced a favorable result in that the organizations represented in the partial target system were not able to block the Planning Council's housing review system. I think that had we confronted all elements of the target system simultaneously—particularly if we had dealt with all the local governments without first gaining agreements with HUD— we would have been defeated before we were even ready to begin.

Two general recommendations regarding the selection of a partial target group can be drawn from our experiences. First, the group should be so constituted as to insure the success of the limited demonstration. That is, it should have some of the following characteristics: receptive to the innovation, generally accepting of change, good relationship with or willingness to work with the practitioner, good motivation, special qualifications such as education, and skills or experiences that would facilitate a successful demonstration.

Second, the partial group should be respected by the general target population (or least not be a deviant, disapproved segment). There should be strong linkages and good means of communication between the partial and general targets. (This second recommendation would not apply when one wanted the demonstration to be a *fait accompli* before diffusing, so as not to arouse a known opposition). The size of the partial target and its *proportional* size relative to the general target should have a bearing on both these matters.

Three, action implications are suggested from other practitioner comments.

Give attention to interpersonal factors.

Practitioners stress the degree to which this guideline calls for the exercise of interpersonal skills with board members, clients, the agency executive, and other people.

> One needs to be clear about the nature and quality of interpersonal relationships involved in the process of trying to reach the goal.

This suggests that the guideline entails modes of influence such as persuasion, example, and communication. It does not typically involve manipulation of power or the use of conflict and contention. As one practitioner puts it, "This approach is useful for getting new ideas accepted that do not have major implications for the existing power relationships."

Determine the amount of environmental support—opposition and obstacles.

Nothing in the guideline itself would automatically alert you to consider very strong influences in the environment. It seems to me that the successful implementation of any innovation would generally require a substantial support in the environment.

The most problematic aspect was securing the resources to conduct the demonstration properly in the first place.

The guideline is a natural approach to innovations which have some support by those who control resources enough to conduct the demonstration. In my situation there are generally enough actors that support can be found for most anything if the timing is right.

My mistake was that I overestimated the need for a program without assessing whether parents really wanted it before having some other needs met.

It may, in some ways, presume an adminstrative structure predisposed to giving sanction to experimentation and trying out new ideas. It requires that the practitioner trying to use it must be very clear about the realities of his authority to effect change, or even do his basic everyday job.

Try the strategy first on a less important issue. After this experience, expand to a larger scale or to more significant innovation.

I feel that working through the goal formulation and operationalizing elements aspects on the initial log was the most problematic of the guideline. Although the examples given were of great value, I still feel one had to have the experience of working it through before it could be understood and of future use.

Perhaps a good way to end this general discussion of the guide-line, and to form a bridge with its actual implementation in the field, is to heed the words of one practitioner:

> Once one determines how the innovation can be experienced ini-tially by the partial group there is little problem in carrying it out.

GETTING STARTED

In attempting to use this guideline for the first time, you might follow this thought-action process:

(1) Think of some new program, technique, or other activity that you have been planning to carry out or that ties in with general tasks and objectives of your current position or assignment.

(2) Attempt to set this down as a goal, but of moderate scope and of short-range time dimension—something that could be completed in a minimum of about 5 and a maximum of 12 weeks.

(3) Conceptualize the general or "total" target system at which this innovation is directed: Who are the people collectively who would be benefiting from utilizing or participating in this innovation?

(4) Think through a smaller segment of that target system, a more delimited subgroup:

(a) Who might relatively easily be drawn into a trial or demonstration of the innovation.

(b) With whom there is a high likelihood of success in an initial trial.

(c) Whose success would be likely to have an impact on the larger target system, or on a relevant Decision-Making Unit that could legitimate or authorize transfer of the innovation to the larger target system.

(5) Early in the game, authorization or legitimation is often needed in order to proceed. This may be obtained from an administrative superordinate (supervisor, agency director, and so on) or from the agency board. Also quite early in the process, persons or organizations may need to be approached who can provide resources to carry through the small-scale demonstration, or can offer access to the smaller target system. Make a determination of the individuals, groups, or organizations whose acceptance needs to be gained.

(6) When you have worked the issue through in your mind to this point, begin to fill out the Initial Log. This is meant to assist you to formulate (put down on paper) some tentative early steps that you might take in starting to carry out this guideline.

I N I T I A L L O G F O R M

As a further step toward getting started, we suggest that you put down your tentative thoughts regarding implementation of the guideline. The Initial Log Form we developed was helpful to practitioners in that connection. The Initial Log is a tool for organizing your thinking in a systematic way. It is geared especially to helping you think about your goal, ways of operationalizing the guideline, the key individual and community groups to involve, and the facilitating and limiting factors in the situation (personal, agency, client, community).

Following the Log Form you will find illustrations of key sections that were completed by guideline users.

INITIAL LOG: A PRELIMINARY GUIDE
FOR ACTION

1. Date of Preparation of Guide for Action _____.

2. In relation to using the guideline, what is your goal (i.e., the innovation)? Be as specific and concrete as possible. Keep a short-term time perspective (five to 12 weeks).

3. Describe the circumstances (conditions, events, assignments, requests, etc.) that led you to use this guideline to achieve the goal above.

4. Look back at the intervention guideline. How would you begin to define or concretize *each* element of the guideline in your immediate practice situation (i.e., how might you operationalize these components)? Keep in mind the delimited innovation goal stated in question 2.

   (a) What is the *General Target System:*

   The Proximate Target:

   (b) What is the Partial Target System (specifically):

   (c) Is a Decision-Making unit involved? Describe it. How will its members be encouraged to accept the innovation?

   (d) How will you foster diffusion from the partial to the larger target—for example, forms of linkage, communication, promotion?

5. List the *major* steps you anticipate going through to utilize this guideline. Describe specific behaviors in the order in which you expect they will occur.

   _____

   _____

   _____

_____

_____

6. What *key* community groups will you probably involve (if any)?

Group   Reason for Contact

_____   _____

_____   _____

_____   _____

_____   _____

_____   _____

7. What *key* individuals will you probably involve (if any)?

	Title and/or	
Individual(s)	Affiliation	Reason for Contact
_____	_____	_____
_____	_____	_____
_____	_____	_____
_____	_____	_____
_____	_____	_____
_____	_____	_____

8. Facilitating and limiting factors in guideline implementation.

As an aid to implementation you should consider factors that will affect your progress. We have provided checklists of common *facilitating factors*, those that will assist you to carry out the guideline, and typical *limiting factors*, those that may inhibit your success. In the checklists we have included conditions that were

frequently indicated by practitioners. Others may be
important in your own situation, and space is provided
for you to note these.

Personal Factors

Facilitating

☐ Good personal relationship with administrator.

☐ Good personal relationship with supervisor.

☐ Good personal relationship with staff.

☐ Personal commitment to the agency.

☐ Personal knowledge of clients.

☐ Personal position or role.

☐ Good personal reputation.

☐ Self-confidence.

☐ Other: _____

_____

Limiting

☐ Poor personal relationship with board (members).

☐ Lack of personal knowledge of the community.

☐ Poor personal reputation.

☐ Personal loss (demotion, job title, etc.).

☐ Overinvolvement.

☐ Fatigue.

☐ Lack of time.

☐ Other: _____

_____

Agency Factors

Facilitating

☐ External authority requires your organization to support your effort.

☐ Affiliated organizational support.

☐ Board involvement.

☐ Administration support or involvement.

☐ Administration disinterest.

☐ Supervisor involvement.

☐ Supervisor disinterest.

☐ Physical facilities aid the effort.

☐ Other: _____

_____

Limiting

☐ Lack of power or authority of your organization.

☐ Unclear or shifting goals, programs, or assignments.

☐ Lack of agency knowledge of clients or community.

☐ Lack of agency support, or hindering action of affiliated organizations.

☐ Lack of agency support, or hindering action of supervisor.

☐ Other: _____

_____

Client Factors

Facilitating

- ☐ Voluntary client participation in your organization or program.

- ☐ Client participation in your organization or program through a legal or administrative ruling.

- ☐ Client is generally interested in your organization.

- ☐ Client shows receptivity to your organization or program.

- ☐ Other: _____

_____

Limiting

- ☐ Client shows a general negative response to your organization.

- ☐ Client is disinterested or dissatisfied with your organizaiton or program.

- ☐ Client lack of knowledge of your organization, its purposes, programs, or activities.

- ☐ Other: _____

_____

Community Factors

Facilitating

☐ Voluntary community participation in your organization or program.

☐ Community support of clients.

☐ Other: _____

_____

Limiting

☐ Community disinterest or dissatisfaction with your organization or program

☐ Community lack of knowledge of your organization, its purposes, programs, or activities.

☐ External influences make the community unsupportive of your organization or program.

☐ Community residents are specifically disinterested in your program.

☐ Other: _____

_____

9. Facilitating factors—relative importance.

In general, to what degree do you think *personal factors related to yourself* may be facilitating in implementing this guideline? (These factors might include good relationships with staff, good relationships with community people, personal knowledge of community, and positive effects of skill.)

Rate the degree of facilitation:

None   0   1   2   3   4   Great Deal

In general, to what degree do you think *agency* factors may be facilitating in implementing this guideline? (These factors might include administration support, supervisor support, staff support, and physical facilities aid effort.)

Rate the degree of facilitation:

None   0   1   2   3   4   Great Deal

In general, to what degree do you think *client* factors may be facilitating in implementing this guideline? (These factors might include client participation in organization or program receptivity to organization of program, client receptivity to organization or program, and client support of practitioner.)

Rate the degree of facilitation:

None   0   1   2   3   4   Great Deal

In general, to what degree do you think *community* factors may be facilitating in implementing this guideline? (These factors might include community support organization generally, influential and other community groups support organization or program, changes in community tend to support organization or program, and community support of practitioner.)

Rate the degree of facilitation:

| None | 0 | 1 | 2 | 3 | 4 | Great Deal |

10. Limiting factors—relative importance.

In general, to what degree do you think *personal factors related to yourself* may be limiting in implementing this guideline? (These factors might include poor relationships with staff, poor relationships with community people, lack of personal knowledge of community, and negative effects of insufficient skill.)

Rate the degree of facilitation:

| None | 0 | 1 | 2 | 3 | 4 | Great Deal |

In general, to what degree do you think *agency* factors may be limiting in implementing this guideline? (These factors might include unclear or shifting goals, programs, and/or assignments; lack of funds, facilities, and other resources; lack of support or hindering action of supervisor; and lack of support or hindering action of staff.)

Rate the degree of facilitation:

| None | 0 | 1 | 2 | 3 | 4 | Great Deal |

In general, to what degree do you think *client* factors may be limiting in implementing this guideline? (These factors might include negative response to organization generally, clients interference with organization activities, and dissensus among clients.)

Rate the degree of facilitation:

| None | 0 | 1 | 2 | 3 | 4 | Great Deal |

In general, to what degree do you think *community* factors may be limiting in implementing this guideline? (These factors might include negative response to organization generally, lack of knowledge of organization purposes, programs, or activities; influential community groups or leaders that do not support organization or program; and competition by other activities with community residents' time and interests.)

Rate the degree of facilitation:

| None | 0 | 1 | 2 | 3 | 4 | Great Deal |

ILLUSTRATIONS OF INITIAL LOGS COMPLETED BY PRACTITIONERS

I. EXAMPLE OF OUTREACH PROGRAMS IN HOUSING PROJECT

A. Goal Statement

To establish outreach services for tenants in a housing project served by a traditional family service agency. (A broader goal, beyond the application to the guideline in this particular instance, is related to a desire for the agency to establish outreach services in the community generally.)

B. Concretization (Operationalization) of Guideline Elements

General Target System: All tenants of the housing project (20 courts)

  The Proximate Target: tenants in six courts

Partial Target System: One court made up of six families. This court will be selected fairly randomly, because there is little basis for knowing which court offers the best potential for successful initial implementation.

II. EXAMPLE OF SOCIAL WELFARE EMPLOYEES UNION

A. Goal Statement

To establish a pattern of implementation of union programs at the building level through building committees at each work location.

B. Concretization (Operationalization) of Guideline
   Elements

General Target System: All building units (25 in all)

> *The Proximate Target:* Six units contiguous to
> one another and to the partial system.

> *Partial Target System*: One building-level committee
> structure where staff has already expressed an
> interest in operating in this way. (This interest can
> be built on to bring about an initial successful trial.)

Notes

1. Everett Rogers of the University of Michigan has codified much of the
   research on innovation in his two books, *The Diffusion of Innovations*
   (New York: Free Press, 1962); and the revised edition with F. Floyd
   Shoemaker, *The Communication of Innovations* (New York: Free Press,
   1971).
2. Richard O. Carlson, "School Superintendents and Adoption of Modern
   Math: A Social Structure Profile," in Matthew B. Miles, ed., *Innovation
   in Education* (New York: Teachers College, Columbia Unity, 1964).
3. Gerald Zaltman, Robert Duncan, and Jonny Holbek, *Innovations and
   Organizations* (New York: Wiley-Interscience, 1973), p. 39.

3

Changing an Organization's Goals

The overwhelming majority of human service practitioners spend their entire professional careers working in one or another organization, and they often work at least in part on behalf of (or in relation to) still other organizations. It is clear that organizational factors set parameters for practice and shape available strategies and programs. Meyer Zald has succinctly stated the practitioner's situation: " 'Needs' and 'problems'. . . are defined and shaped by the employing agency. The techniques selected to deal with them also depend upon requirements of the organization. Whether the practitioner facilitates, fund raises, or foments, whether he plans, serves as a resource expert, counsels, or agitates is determined by the structure, aims and operating procedures of the organization that pays the bill."[1] The collective welfare of practitioners' clients and constituents is profoundly affected by the organizational structures and goals of social agencies. Changing an organization's goals thus becomes a key task for many practitioners, and failure to accomplish this objective is frequently a great hindrance to effective practice.

The chairman of a welfare workers union took on this task when he decided to move his organization toward more "radical" or working class goals:

> What I wanted to do was to further develop the working class orientation and efforts of the union. Not that the constitution did not permit such a direction. It's just that the way the organization actually operated, its goals were more along a trade union model than a working class one. The trade union approach emphasizes strictly bread and butter issues such as wages, workload, work speedup, and the like. I wanted to incorporate the notion of working class interests that went beyond the local job situation. For example, finding solidarity with clients as fellow workers and with other peoples' movements. This means that sure we would be concerned about bread and butter issues, but would also go beyond them—link up with clients' rights groups and other grassroots organizations, take a more pro-client position, protect workers who engage in protest actions with clients, etc.

Unfortunately, organizations usually are less than enthusiastic about intervention overtures directed at them. Morris and Binstock have described the problem this way:

> For a number of reasons, organizations are predisposed to resist changes embodied in social planning goals. . . . The propensity of organizations to resist . . . poses important practical questions for the planner. Is it possible to predict or anticipate which target agencies are especially likely to resist? How extensively?
>
> No classification has yet been developed which provides systematic guidance for predictions as to which organization, under what circumstances, will resist certain types of planning goals. . . . For the present, social planners must rely upon a sensitive reading of each new situation against an extensive backdrop of relatively intimate knowledge of the pertinent organizations.[2]

In this chapter, we want to help the practitioner to move beyond intuitive, ad hoc engagements with organizations by spelling out at least one potentially effective means of influencing an organization's goals.

RESEARCH ON ORGANIZATIONS' GOALS

Our review of the existing research on organization' goals has yielded the following useful generalization:

> An organization's dominant goals reflect the influences of the most powerful individuals or groups in the organization and their vested interests.[3]

For example, in a university setting described by Gross,[4] goals such as academic freedom, developing student intellect and creativity, preserving the cultural heritage, and pure research are emphasized in organizations where the faculty has more power than other groups. However, in universities controlled by legislatures or the state government, emphasis is placed on goals such as service to the community and vocational or technical training.

From this generalization relating goals to interests and values of power groups we have derived the action guideline:

> Practitioners wishing to change an organization's goals may approach this problem by altering the structure of influence within the organization by either: (a) increasing the power of those groups within the organization that hold goals compatible with the practitioner's or (b) introducing new groups into the organization that hold goals compatible with the practitioner's

This guideline embodies a structural and "political" orientation to organizational change. The supposition in applying this guideline

is that the "powers that be"—agency director, board, supervisors—
are not in sympathy with the goal change. This is not uniformly so.
In some instances the executive may be highly innovative and a
major resource for change. Occasionally the practitioner may become allied with the executive in promoting goals that are opposed
at higher policy levels. Other types of initiatives may be taken—for
example, persuasion, use of outside consultants, selected focus
groups—when there is a reasonable amount of common purpose
and consensus on values among the various actors and interests in
the situation. This basic strategy is thus only one of several available alternatives.

An illustration is contained in Mehina and Perrow's study of a
youth commission in a local midwestern city.[5] This commission had
been established to recommend new programs to deal with the city's
youth problems, but it actually performed as a clearing house and
was devoid of activity or programs. The study indicated that the
commission's inactivity stemmed from overlapping memberships;
that is, most of its members belonged to other youth organizations
that were not interested in the development of new, competitive
efforts in this field. Only after citizens without ties to existing youth
organizations were added to the commission did it begin to initiate
specific programs.

In addition to offering strategies for action, the guideline also
provides a diagnostic tool. That is, practitioners may be aided in
identifying dominant goals at any given time if they assess the
interests of the most powerful groups in the organizations.

Parsons has observed that a task-related, primary orientation
toward the attainment of specific goals is "the defining character-
istic of an organization which distinguishes it from other types of
social systems."[6] In this sense, an organization cannot be understood, or worked with, without reference to its goals. Two observations should be useful in analyzing organizations and their goals.

First, *most organizations have multiple goals rather than a single goal.* A useful schema for viewing agencies from a multiple-goal framework is offered by Perrow,[7] who distinguishes six types of goals.

(1) *societal goals,* which relate to an organization's efforts to mobilize legitimation for its existence from the larger society. (Example: A clinic for drug-addicted youth that wishes to obtain legitimation from the larger society—a legitimation that may ensure financial support—may emphasize its possible contribution to the solution of the general drug problem.)

(2) *output goals,* which relate to the public constituency or clientele of the organization, that is, to the groups that directly receive the organization's outputs or benefits. (Example: Help provided by the aforementioned clinic to drug-addicted youth.)

(3) *investor goals,* which relate to the return that the investors, such as contributors, board members, or volunteers, receive for their investments of time or money in the organization. (Example: Individuals may receive favorable newspaper mention, for instance, for assisting the clinic in its work.).

(4) *system goals,* which relate to the organization's efforts to maintain its own equilibrium and stability. (Example: Activities designed to ensure a solid resource base for the organization—money and professional manpower, for instance.)

(5) *product goals,* which relate to the specific "product" of the organization. (Example: In the case of a welfare department, the client's checks. In human service organizations, many output goals are the same as product goals.)

(6) *derived goals*, which relate to functions that have only an indirect relation to the organization's main goals. (Example: In the case of the clinic, its involvement in civil rights activities that many of the clients support.)

In designating a goal to change, then, a practitioner must specify which of multiple goals is being singled out for attention. An organization may be differentially subject to influence, based on which subgoal (or subgoals) is delineated as the target of intervention.

Second, *organizations' goals are not static; they shift over time.* In sociologists' terms, what takes place is either "goal displacement" (substituting one goal for another) or "goal succession" (adding new goals when old ones have been realized or cannot be attained).

Zald and Denton's examination of the YMCA[8] illustrates how an organization shifts its goals in order to adjust to a new social environment and thereby protects its survival. The original goals of the Y included improving the social conditions of lower class people through religious indoctrination and educational activities. Over time, these goals broadened to include more general all-purpose service activities aimed at middle as well as lower class people.

A useful illustration of a shift in an organization's goal emphasis is provided by Perrow[9] in his study of voluntary general hospitals. He shows how changes in organizational needs modify the composition of internal goals. When the hospitals needed financial resources, the trustees were the dominant group that shaped major goals. The situation changed, however, after the organization's financial situation became secure and the need for professional prestige emerged. Domination in the organization was then transferred to the medical staff. With the development and expansion of hospitals, however, the need for coordinating complex functions, including interdependent and specialized health services, paved the way for domination by the administrative staff. Focal organizational goals may be viewed, therefore, as phases that dominate and fade according to organizational needs. Equally significant, different organizational factions may attain varying level of influence as goals shift over time.

It may be useful to view an organization's goals from a historical perspective, in order to assess dysfunctional goals that have been inadvertently adopted, as well as to make use of natural trends and tendencies in transformation of goals.

OPERATIONALIZING THE GUIDELINE

This guideline has four components: (1) changing an organization's goals; (2) altering the structure of influence; and either (3) increasing the power of groups already functioning in the organization or (4) introducing new groups into the organization. We have discussed goals in the previous section. Now we shall examine the action components.

ALTERING THE STRUCTURE OF INFLUENCE

There may be many centers of power or influence in an organization: an agency's board, the executive, the staff, membership or clientele, or community elites. Furthermore, different groups may be influential for achieving different goals. Thus, to change a particular goal, one might need to make a shift within a particular group (for example, certain program goals may be changed by shifts within the staff; procedural goals by shifts within the administration; and policy goals by sifts within the board). On the other hand, to change another goal might necessitate a shift in influence from one group to another (for example, strengthening the hand of the staff as opposed to the board). In the case of the welfare workers union referred to at the beginning of the chapter, the chairman shifted a particular segment of the membership into a stronger position within the leadership or decision-making hierarchy:

> The question I had to deal with was the nature of the relationship between organizational goals and power distribution within the organization. What I set out to do was to increase the relative power of the black members and of the non-college degree holding members of the organization. Conversely the power of the white members of the organization would be decreased, as would that of the college degree holding members. In a general sense, the race and the class variables converged. The majority of the blacks did not hold college degrees while the majority of the whites did have BA's. At the outset, the power of the whites in the organization was disproportionately high in relation to their numbers. In this context it was specifically attempted to increase the power of the non-college degree holding blacks by increasing their ability and opportunity to move into leadership positions within the organization. This educational component was vital in this process.
>
> Not all members of the non-college work forces were sympathetic to a working class point of view. In fact some of the more conflictual relationships in the whole agency were between clerical staff and clients. My concern was that by altering the power within the organization (increasing the power of the non-professionals) I might set in motion a process of unwanted organizational goal changes through giving leadership to even more conservative elements. This did not happen. To ensure that it did not happen, a strong educational component was included which involved both those who would be increasing their relative power and those who would have less. We set up a "labor school" program to which we invited the entire membership. At the same time we did active recruiting among those members of the non-college, black staff who we knew had a progressive attitude and who had been critical of the organization for functioning as a traditional trade union.

The training program dealt with subjects such as the history of the labor movement in the United States and Europe, the rise of militant unionism during the Depression, blacks and labor unions and shop "floor" strategy. Training was used as a means of increasing the effectiveness of those who viewed the union from a working class perspective. This did two things. First, it created a feeling of confidence that we really meant business in implementing the stated working class goals of the union. Second, it provided folks with more expertise in operating as organizers at their place of work.

A real risk of this guideline (in organizations like mine) is that the perceived loss of influence by those whose relative power is declining can result in their taking divisive actions which cause the splintering or disintegration of the organization. In this instance, if that had occurred, it might well have taken on racial overtones as well as class conflict (this happened only on an individual basis and involved only two people). It is for this reason that a great deal of priority was placed on the educational component, involving both those who were losing power and those who were gaining power. That is to say, the decision to proceed with the educational program was made democratically and everyone was invited to participate through a general mailing to the entire membership.

We are now in a much better position to continue moving in this direction. We have already established definite linkages with welfare reform and welfare rights groups. Levels of antagonism between clerical staff and clients are being reduced. With time the effect of the new leadership should produce some very important payoffs in better services for clients as well as in the development of a more relevant and powerful union.

The type of organizational structure involved affects the choice of approaches to the influence system. For example, in a "rationalistic" organization, one that has the classic top-to-bottom authority structure typical of formal bureaucracies, it may be essential to influence the director, board, or some other level higher than the one at which a change is sought. On the other hand, in a "human relations" type of organization, which has a diffuse or decentralized authority structure with decisions made among the workers themselves, it may be necessary to achieve a staff rather than an executive decision. In some professional organizations, personnel cherish their autonomy and are not likely to conscientiously carry out directives handed to them from above.

Influence in an organization may be a subtle and complex phenomenon. The idea behind this guideline is that influence should be sufficient to affect a goal in a particular direction. A shift in influence may in one instance require a formal modification of the authority structure of the organization, perhaps through a change in the bylaws. In another case a staff group may be brought together informally and, by speaking with a unified voice, may force the agency director to steer a different course. The point is that power and influence may be formal or informal, *de jure* or *de facto*, depending on the situation and the objective.

This guideline has a branching aspect—a kind of fork in the road—with a choice of two courses of action. A shift of influence may be executed either through *internal adjustments alone* or through the introduction of *new elements from outside the organization*. While both logic and experience suggest that both may be used simultaneously, for purposes of an orderly presentation we will treat them as separate alternatives.

INCREASING THE POWER OF GROUPS WITHIN THE ORGANIZATION

Often it is possible for the practitioner to find factions of the organization who are in sympathy with her aims. The task, then, is to strengthen the status, resources, or formal decision-making roles of these groups. In the example of the welfare workers' union, members with a working class orientation were singled out as a compatible intraorganizational faction. Through a training program these people were provided access to leadership roles in the organization.

Of course, as the practitioner stated, there is always the danger of a reaction by the people whose influence is proportionately reduced. As in any "political" strategy, this countervailing potential has to be anticipated and taken into account in the primary and contingency strategy measures being used. In the example, the chairman neutralized the potential reaction by having the training program adopted openly by the organization as a whole and by publicly inviting the participation of all people (while privately actively recruiting among the progressive faction).

Other strategies for increasing the power of sympathetic groups within an agency are illustrated by the experiences of two practitioners, one working in a family service agency and the other in a regional planning council:

Family Service Agency. My specific goal in using the guideline was to use the mental retardation program as a wedge in the agency and through it to move to a position of advocacy. My particular methodology was a slow process, but it is on the way to working now.

Altering the structure of influence—an element in this guideline—could be accomplished by introducing new people and new ideas to the board. I decided to do this through my program committee: the advisory committee on mental retardation. This was a new group in the agency which embraced the advocacy position, and had access to the board through the committee chairman, a board member. It was a board-appointed committee and at the board level, but board committees were often only pro forma. To move toward accomplishing my objective took some real planning. Initially, I had to be sure that the mental retardation committee accepted the advocacy position, and did this by submitting to them a "proposed" set of committee objectives which included advocacy. They not only accepted it, but strengthened it.

A device I used was to make sure that our mental retardation committee chairman always has something to report at the board meetings. This served to create an awareness about our group on the part of the board, so that when issues arose, the board would listen.

As yet we have not had a chance to test the "issue" idea, but we did get listened to with much interest. I have no doubt but that the question of advocacy can and will be raised through this committee given time and the right conditions.

Regional Planning Council. The Federal Office of Management and Budget requires that state and regional planning agencies review federal grant applications for a number of programs, including housing. The Regional Planning Council performed these reviews in a very perfunctory fashion. A long-time and fairly traditional planner had handled this responsibility for the Council and had been assisted by a technical advisory committee appointed by the board, largely composed of county planners and other city and state officials who were content to keep the Council in a relatively passive role. I and a couple of other Council staff members also were official participants of the ad hoc committee.

My objective in terms of this guideline was to change the Council's implicit organizational goal of a perfunctory, passive review of housing applications to a more aggressive policy which has the goal of actively influencing the housing situation. In the past, for example, grant applications were reviewed only in comparison with existing regional plans. (If a proposed highway was in conflict with the regional highway plan it would be rejected.) I wanted to expand housing reviews to take into account a number of humanistic criteria, which although not yet part of a formalized regional plan, were important factors to consider in the development of housing programs. Such criteria include the community's need for the income level of housing proposed, equal housing opportunities to be offered, etc. In order to attain this goal change, I felt that I would have to revise the balance of decision-making process within the Council, shifting the weight of influence from those who favored an inert role to those who favored an assertive role. I felt that this goal change would not be accepted by the advisory committee, given the policies followed and the membership of the committee.

My strategy therefore was to avoid bringing up housing reviews before the committee. I was able to do this as a result of certain delays produced by negotiating problems in the Council's dealings with HUD. I kept telling the committee members that we would consider the housing reviews in a separate appendix of the general review manual which the committee was preparing. Finally, the committee disbanded before any matters relating to housing were decided.

In the meantime, I had been conferring with some Council staff members, including the deputy director, who I believed would favor a more out-front housing policy. Based on my discussions with the staff program heads of such areas as transportation, environmental health, education, and recreation, the deputy director decided that my proposal for a more-encompassing housing review policy to be conducted by selected staff would be accepted by the agency.

Thus I believe that by shifting the balance of influence away from the board advisory committee and to an informal set of persons composed of certain agency program heads and the deputy director, I was able to change the organizational goals of the Council with regard to housing in the region.

(An interesting twist in interpretation was used in the second example. In this case, the power of one group was reduced or phased out prior to the shift of influence to an alternate group. This pattern may reduce some of the resistance and opposition that is likely to occur when the shift is simultaneous.)

INTRODUCING NEW GROUPS INTO THE ORGANIZATION

Sometimes a practitioner may find that no groups in the organization favor the goals he is pursuing or that the supporting groups are weak. One attractive course of action is to engage in educational work within the organization in order to build one or more clusters of support or strength. Another is to introduce new groups into the

organization with compatible values and objectives. These new
groups might be board members, staff, or clients. It may be especially useful to draw on the "outside" strategy when particular
outside influences are implicated in the desired goal change or when
the target agency has strong interdependent relationships with external units. Within the general format of a political strategy, this
external approach is probably more threatening, volatile, and risky
(essentially, more "political") than the internal one. Perhaps for this
reason few project practitioners used this option. One who did, a
worker in a neighborhood service center, met with some success:

> While the Neighborhood Service Center was supposed to be ser-
> vicing the needs of the poor in our geographic area, the preschool
> program was definitely reaching primarily middle class families.
> Mothers were using our center to dump kids for a morning or an
> afternoon while they went shopping or played bridge. I felt that
> we ought to drop this activity so that the resources could be
> shifted to assist the target population of poor residents. Part of
> the problem in changing the situation was that some of the middle
> class black and white board members were intent on preserving
> this program, since it was one of the few integrated ones the center
> was running. I decided to use the guideline to try and institute
> some changes in the present mode of operations.
>
> I met with my supervisor to discuss my idea and also to seek
> support and approval. After this meeting, I proceeded to arrange
> a meeting with the Director of the Child Care Federation of the
> county. We discussed what I wanted to do, the information I
> wanted from her, and the role I wanted her to play. I got what
> information I needed and proceeded to contact directors of day
> care centers to get additional information. After collecting, ana-
> lyzing, and writing this up, I gave it to my supervisor for approval
> and suggestions.
>
> At this point I was asked to arrange for the Child Care Fed-
> eration Director to attend the program committee with us. At the

meeting all of us presented information, and the Federation Director stressed the needs of the poor, but no final decision was
made. . . . Later the matter was referred to the entire board with
a suggestion from the program committee that the program be
discontinued as it is and other alternatives be sought. (The program was subsequently discontinued.)

So far we have given four examples of how our project
practitioners implemented this guideline. In Figure 3.1 (page 64),
these narratives are summarized under the headings of the
guidelines four components.

PATTERNS OF IMPLEMENTATION

As we have seen in implementing this guideline, a practitioner has
a choice of two means, either shifting the influence of groups within
the agency or introducing new groups into the agency. In addition,
the context of this action may be either his own agency or an external agency. Thus there are four possible patterns of implementation, which may be seen most easily in a simple four-cell table:

MEANS	CONTEXT	
	Own Agency	*External Target Agency*
Shifting influence of groups within the agency	a	c
Introducing new groups into the agency	b	d

Setting	Changing an Organization's Goals	Altering Structure of Influence within the Organization	Increasing Powers of Groups within the Organization that Hold Goals Compatible with the Practitioner
Welfare Workers Union	From traditional trade union goals to working class orientation goals	Shifting progressive black members into the leadership, decision-making structure	Giving progressive black members training, increasing their expertise, and bringing them into leadership roles
Regional Planning Council	From passive housing review policy to active housing review policy	Phasing out the Board appointed review committee and setting up an informal staff review group	Assigning responsibility for housing review decision to the new informal staff group
Family Service Agency	From traditional in-house service policy to out-reach	Increasing the influence of a board-appointed committee	Making the board-appointed committee more active in its pro-advocacy input into the board
			Introducing New Groups into the Organization that Hold Goals Compatible with the Practitioners
Neighborhood Service Center	Eliminate day-care program serving a middle class clientele	Introducing new authoritative information into program committee deliberations	Having director of Child Care Federation take part in program committee deliberations

Figure 3.1: Elements of the Goal Change Guideline Operationalized

As we have already noted, making internal changes is more manageable and tends to be less political than introducing new elements into an organization. And it is easier and safer to work within one's own agency than to try to change an external organization. As one moves through the cells from *a* to *b* to *c* to *d*, the task becomes less controllable and riskier, and accessibility becomes more difficult.

In the cell *a* pattern (own agency, "inside" strategy), the locus of influence being affected may be the board or executive group, the executive staff, the operating or program staff, the organization members, or the agency clients. For a practitioner, the board may be the most difficult locus and the staff perhaps the easiest in terms of accessibility and manipulability. As we indicated earlier, shifts may take place within one group, or from one group to another. In the example of the family service agency, the shift of influence took place within the board. In the case of the regional planning council, the staff gained influence at the expense of the board.

The cell *b* pattern (own agency, "outside" strategy), was followed by the practitioner in our example of the neighborhood service center. He chose to bring a single individual from the outside (an "expert") into the situation in order to influence the board in the desired direction. While relying on an individual rather than a group was effective here, in another case the selected individual was not able to follow through, and the entire effort collapsed. Working through a group may be more difficult and time-consuming in some ways, but it also may be a safer way to proceed. Outside elements may also be injected at the staff or membership-client levels of an organization depending on the type of decision one is attempting to effect and on who has the power to make that decision.

In another case a school-community agent working in an elementary school used several external trainers (a group of experts) to influence teachers to accept certain curriculum wishes of low-income parents.

As with other guidelines, you should capitalize on the facilitating factors in the situation.

In the personal area, it would be well to choose a goal change that falls within your position or role in the agency. This may provide a certain level of legitimation for your activities and permit a concentration of effort. It may be helpful if the action grows out of your prior experiences, so that this, too, can be applied toward optimizing the outcome. If possible, pick a program to which you have some commitment. You should take care to maintain good working relationships with staff members, administrators, and board members. Patience is not a particular virtue in implementing this guideline. Commitment rather than patience, practitioners state, is the important consideration when aiming at short-term, proximate goal changes. Choose a goal that is of interest to the client group or to which they are receptive. As an alternative, make it your business to work on building such interest and receptivity.

In the community, disinterest or dissatisfaction are useful facilitating factors. Such dissatisfaction may provide background pressure that stimulates change and enables client involvement to have an impact. You may select a goal in an area in which such dissatisfaction or disinterest already exists or attempt to develop a sense of dissatisfaction in the community as part of the implementation strategy.

In the agency sector it is facilitating if the intervention is consistent with your already assigned tasks. Again, legitimation and concentration of energy may be the operating variables here. It is useful to obtain the support of staff and, perhaps, to a lesser degree, that of supervisors. During implementation it may appear helpful to have administration support also. However, administrators may block goal changes in the end for various reason having to do with use of resources or the politics of the situation, for example.

The greatest limitations may be anticipated in the agency and personal sectors. Agency structural factors may be a special problem, particularly unclear or shifting goals. Perhaps it is possible to turn the fluidity of such a situation to an advantage by approaching it as an occasion that provides openings for the introduction of new goals. Lack of resources is another inhibiting factor. It may be useful to seek out possible resource inputs from outside sources (such as other agencies with similar objectives). Availability of such external resources is likely to remove important resistances to adopting some types of new goals.

On the personal side, pressures of time, involvement, and fatigue may inhibit movement. The principle of concentration of energy applies here. It is important for community practitioners to use their time efficiently, to set priorities, and to eliminate less productive involvements.

Clients are not likely to be a problem, competition of other activities for their time and interest constituting perhaps the greatest difficulty. This suggests selecting a goal that is salient to clients or working to stir up such interest. At the same time other educational work with clients may be needed in providing either background knowledge about the organization or program, or skills necessary to the carrying out of certain client roles. The same types of difficulties may be anticipated from the wider community, and similar approaches should be considered at the community level. Lack of community funds may turn out not to be as large a problem as it appears during implementation and should not be a deterrent to moving ahead.

Let us now look at more narrative comments of practitioners.

PRACTITIONERS' VIEWS OF PROBLEMS AND PROSPECTS

Changing goals of organizations is obviously an important part of community practice. At the same time, this is extremely difficult to accomplish. Practitioners run into many obstacles and resistances in implementing this guideline.

What our practitioners say is that the strategy is potentially very effective, but that it also may be political, controversial, and hazardous. A succinct summary of the views of many is contained in these comments by three practitioners:

(1) I think that this is important because it offers possibilities whenever a practitioner is blocked in the system. He has the option of changing from the inside or attempting to do what I did in bringing someone in who may have an impact.

(2) This guideline seems to allow for considerable potential change, while also necessitating some risk for the practitioner in the area of power politics and group conflict.

(3) Some changes carry the concept of "winners" and "losers" within them. It requires some study as to how to achieve a balance so that more is not lost than is gained. Decreasing the influence of certain groups may be a source of future conflict.

Some practitioners obviously find this realm personally threatening or incompatible with their professional philosophy.

> The political aspects of it made me feel uncomfortable because I am much more accustomed to using persuasion.

Practitioners speak also of various benefits they see in using this guideline:

> I consistently find myself in practice situations that warrant goal change. I think that when a practitioner is in an agency setting he must attempt to change the goals if he finds them counterproductive.

Practitioners indicate that demonstrated capability in performing this function can serve as a sign of competence, both to oneself and to others.

> I feel that this guideline can definitely help practitioners new and old to the job establish themselves and feel more comfortable if they are truly able to change an organization's goals to be more in keeping with their own. It is an excellent measure of a practitioner's effectiveness if he is able to effect the organization's goals.

One value of the guideline is that it offers a *diagnostic tool* for assessing what is actually happening in organizational settings.

> It lays out some basic truths about institutions and gives one a handle on thinking about the system.

Even if the guideline is employed unsuccessfully on the first try, the experience and diagnostic skills gained can carry over and be the basis for a more successful second implementation.

> I have no reservations in using this guideline again. I think I will be able to diagnose the situation much better and not use it as a threat to the power group as I think it became this time.

The three most common types of problems pointed out by practitioners as a result of their experience revolved around time considerations, the selection of obtainable objectives, and the practitioner's position in the hierarchy of the organization.

TIME

The problem cited most often was the large amount of time needed to bring about even a small change in an organization's goals. One practitioner noted that the next time he uses the guideline, he will give himself "a much longer period of time to carry it out, realizing the difficulty of dealing with the goals of an organization." And over this long period of time, a great deal of the community worker's time must be committed to the effort. One's schedule has to be adjusted and cleared for the task:

> It is clearly possible to change organizational goals as this guideline indicates. Practitioners, however, are well aware that doing so may add to their work unless some other assignments are eliminated—or subordinated. It adds new volume to an already heavy workload.

Even after the changes are effected, the followup activities may be demanding. One practitioner warns:

> The group that loses influence is likely to become incensed. This means that there will be a lot of "mopping up" to do afterward, a lot of effort put in toward helping the two groups learn to respect each other and work together on the new basis.

OBTAINABLE OBJECTIVES

Practitioners caution that one must be practical in choosing an objective. It is not necessary (and often not desirable) to set out to change the entire organization's goals. It is possible to partialize either the organization (changing only one department) or the goals (attacking only one of an organization's many goals or part of a particular goal). From their experience, practitioners recommended both approaches:

> I would advise that staff using this guideline take on a portion at a time. In other words, do not try to take on the whole organization at once or do it alone. Other people may have ideas as good. Form coalitions when possible.

Again, I would caution workers to change goals that they have easy access to. In other words, take the mountain a piece at a time. In this instance I was successful and that gives me a positive feeling about using it again. It would have been tricky if we were trying to change larger organizational goals.

Feasibility also involves assessing the power of the group you are attempting to influence. In one instance, an agency director was concerned about a conservative executive committee that dominated the board. He wished to change the organization's goals in the direction of more service-oriented programs by enhancing the position of certain members of the board who were not part of the executive clique. He drew these members together in a small group that he hoped would be a countervailing force, but he had not fully recognized the ability of the executive elite to crush a weak opposition. The practitioner summed up his experience as follows:

> I think this guideline can be most useful when there is a willingness on the part of the power group to respect the position and contributions of the newly developed group. It was not helpful with a group that had extreme power and knew how to manipulate behind the scenes and to discredit others.

POSITION IN THE HIERARCHY

Many of the practitioners felt impotent when trying to influence their organization on the level of goal formulation. This was particularly true of younger or less experienced workers (although we saw in the previous illustration that even an agency director is not immune to frustration on this account).

The practitioners suggested two approaches to overcoming this obstacle. First, it may be possible to work through some other individual who has greater authority. If he collaborates with such an individual, the practitioner can take a back seat, allowing a qualified substitute to function in his place. In a certain sense such a strategy involves persuading and training a stronger ally to carry out the action principle of the guideline.

The other suggestion involves selecting an existing and accessible focus of power within the agency, rather than attempting to institute an entirely new center of influence. A practitioner explained his successful implementation:

> In my situation, I made use of latent power of a group already
> formed (and it was a very small goal).

A review of implementation by practitioners who did not have high administrative posts suggests two sources of strength for lower level workers. One is the control and use of information as an instrument of power; the other is mobilization of the staff from a latent to an active force in the organization. From its frequency of occurrence, it would appear that control of information is a type of power available to most practitioners. It appears in such varied circumstances as the gathering and provision of data on child care services, the release of budget information to a staff cohort, the presentation of the results of a student survey to a board of education, and the development of an information system for the juvenile courts. In other words, connecting up new information with newly formed power blocs seems to be a useful way to accumulate a "critical mass" of influence.

In several instances the staff was able to influence goals after the practitioner had helped them to consolidate around a particular objective. As one practitioner analyzed his situation:

> Our staff had compatible goals, but we had not used our power
> as a group before. It became a matter of getting them to act as
> a unit, which gave us more power than if we had taken action as
> individual members.

In this instance, the practitioner was able to build upon previous relationships and staff consensus and was assisted by a critical issue (the arbitrary shifting of office space by a superordinate) to develop a sense of solidarity among the group. Unionization epitomizes this idea, but the concept can also be applied in a less formal way, and with regard to ad hoc situations. Very few staff groups, apparently, maximize the impact they could have were they to operate in a collective fashion.

In addition to these three major areas, a few other problems were identified. One practitioner noted that sometimes there are no compatible groups within the organization with which to align oneself. It may be necessary to abandon this guideline in such a situation, or perhaps to shift to the outside strategy. Even when new groups are introduced into an organization, they may gain no real influence on the organization's goals. This again points up the need for careful diagnostic thinking in designing a plan of implementation.

A middle-level supervisor in a mental health clinic attempted to use the staff as a wedge in moving the director toward serving neglected groups. She encountered difficulties in convincing the staff that she was an ally with a mutual interest in improving the quality of services. It took time for trust to be established across hierarchy levels. Another practitioner in a juvenile court setting found numerous enclaves of people from different disciplines. She underestimated the effort required to get people to cross professional boundaries and form a new common interest staff group.

GETTING STARTED

First, think of some situation or problem in your practice situation that could be improved through a change in organizational goals. The goal should be modest in scope, not involving the entire organization, but perhaps a specific program, activity, or department.

This permits modification of the goal to take place within a three-month period. (The organization may be your own or an external target agency.)

Second, what type of goal is involved among multiple organizational goals? Has this goal been in flux historically? Can the direction of change be capitalized on?

Third, what locus of organizational operation is instrumental in maintaining or changing this goal: board, the executive staff, operating staff, members, clients, and so on?

Fourth, are there individuals or groups in the agency who are in tune with your desired goals? Are they situated close to the primary locus of influence or at another locus?

Fifth, how can the power or influence of these groups be strengthened? Is a shift from one locus to another necessary? How can the power or influence of the people in the current critical locus be reduced, either prior to or simultaneously with a shift of influence to the new group?

Sixth, if there are no such internal groups, are there external groups of this type? Can they be moved into relevant positions of influence within the organization?

Seventh, how can the reaction of current power holders be neutralized or minimized during the transition process?

Eighth, how can the influence of the new group be stabilized or institutionalized?

Ninth, when the transference of influences has been achieved, have the desired changes in goal orientation been realized?

I N I T I A L   L O G   F O R M

As a further step toward getting started, we suggest that you put down your tentative thoughts on the implementation of the guideline. The Initial Log is tool for organizing your thinking in a systematic way. It is geared especially to helping you think about your goal, ways of operationalizing the guideline, the key individual and community groups to involve, and the facilitating and limiting factors in the situation (personal, agency, client, community). Following the Log Form you will find illustrations of key sections that were completed by guideline users.

INITIAL LOG: A PRELIMINARY GUIDE FOR ACTION

1. Date of Preparation of Guide for Action _____.

2. In relation to using the guideline, what is your objective (i.e., the organization goal you wish to change-from, or to)? Keep a short-term time perspective (five to 12 weeks); the *proximate* goal should be indicated.

3. Describe the circumstances (conditions, events, assignments, requests, etc.) that led you to use this guideline to achieve the goal above.

4. Look back at the intervention guideline. How would you begin to define or concretize *each* element of the guideline in your immediate practice situation (i.e., how might you operationalize these components)? Keep in mind the proximate goal stated in question 2.

   How do you intend to alter the structure of influence?

   Will this be brought about by increasing the power of those groups *within* the organization holding compatible goals with the practitioners. Specify.

   Or will it be brought about by introducing new groups into the organization that hold compatible goals with the practitioner's. Specify.

5. List the *major* steps you anticipate going through in
   order to utilize this guideline. Describe specific
   behaviors in the order in which you expect they will
   occur.

   _____

   _____

   _____

   _____

   _____

6. What *key* community groups will you probably involve
   (if any)?

   Group   Reason for Contact

   _____   _____

   _____   _____

   _____   _____

   _____   _____

   _____   _____

7. What *key* individuals will you probably involve (if any)?

| | Title and/or | |
Individual(s)	Affiliation	Reason for Contact
_____	_____	_____
_____	_____	_____
_____	_____	_____
_____	_____	_____
_____	_____	_____

8. Facilitating and limiting factors in guideline implementation.

As an aid to implementation you should consider factors that will affect your progress. We have provided checklists of common *facilitating factors*, those that will assist you to carry out the guideline, and typical *limiting factors*, those that may inhibit your success. In the checklists we have included conditions that were frequently indicated by practitioners. Others may be important in your own situation, and space is provided for you to note these.

Personal Factors

Facilitating

☐ Good personal relationships with board/board members.

☐ Good personal relationship with administrator.

☐ Good personal relationship with supervisor.

☐ Good personal relationships with staff.

☐ Good personal relationships with clients.

☐ Good personal relationships with community people.

☐ Good personal relationships with nonstaff professional peers and friends

☐ Positive effects of commitment to agency.

☐ Positive effects of commitment to program.

☐ Positive effects of commitment to guideline.

☐ Other: _____

_____

Limiting

- ☐ Poor relationships with board/board members.
- ☐ Poor relationships with staff.
- ☐ Negative effects of lack of commitment to agency.
- ☐ Personal knowledge of community.
- ☐ Personal knowledge of clients.
- ☐ Personal loss (demotion, job title, etc.).
- ☐ Negative effects of not enjoying the job.
- ☐ Fatigue.
- ☐ Other: _____

_____

Agency Factors

Facilitating

- ☐ External authority requirements of organization support effort.
- ☐ Affiliated organizational support or involvement.
- ☐ Board support or involvement.
- ☐ Administration support or involvement.
- ☐ Administration disinterest.
- ☐ Supervisor disinterest.
- ☐ Staff involvement.
- ☐ Practitioner assignments are consistent with effort.
- ☐ Physical facilities aid the effort.
- ☐ Other: _____

_____

Limiting

☐ External authority requirements hamper efforts.

☐ Lack of power and/or authority of organization.

☐ Hindering structure of organization.

☐ Negative agency attitudes toward the clients or community.

☐ Lack of knowledge of clients or community.

☐ Lack of staff or training.

☐ Lack of support of board.

☐ Lack of support of administration.

☐ Lack of support of supervisor.

☐ Other: _____

_____

Client Factors

Facilitating

☐ Client support of other clients.

☐ Client support of practitioner.

☐ Other: _____

_____

Limiting

☐ Dissensus among clients

☐ Other: _____

_____

Community Factors

Facilitating

☐ Community participation in your organization or program (through legal or administrative ruling)

☐ Community support of your organization generally.

☐ Community interest in your program specifically.

☐ Support of (influential) community groups for your organizaiton or program.

☐ Influential or other community groups involved with organization or program.

☐ Community disinterest in, or dissatisfaction with, organization or program (leading to a desire for change).

☐ Changes in community tend to support organization or program.

☐ External influences making the community support your organization or program.

☐ Community support of clients.

☐ Other: _____

Limiting

☐ Pressure from community residents

☐ External influences make community unsupportive of organization or program

☐ Community residents not interested in program specifically.

☐ Differences in life styles between staff (incuding practitioner) and community residents

☐ Other: _____

9. Facilitating factors—relative importance.

In general, to what degree do you think *personal factors related to yourself* may be facilitating in implementing this guideline? (These factors might include good relationships with staff, good relationships with community people, personal knowledge of community, and positive effects of skill.)

Rate the degree of facilitation:

None	0	1	2	3	4	Great Deal
___	__	__	__	__	__	

In general, to what degree do you think *agency* factors may be facilitating in implementing this guideline? (These factors might include administration support, supervisor support, staff support, and physical facilities aid effort.)

Rate the degree of facilitation:

None	0	1	2	3	4	Great Deal
___	__	__	__	__	__	

In general, to what degree do you think *client* factors may be facilitating in implementing this guideline? (These factors might include client participation in organization or program receptivity to organization of program, and client support of practitioner.)

Rate the degree of facilitation:

None	0	1	2	3	4	Great Deal
___	__	__	__	__	__	

In general, to what degree do you think *community* factors may be facilitating in implementing this guideline? (These factors might include community support organization generally, influential and other community groups support organization or program, changes in community tend to support organization or program, and community support of practitioner.)

Rate the degree of facilitation:

None   0   1   2   3   4   Great Deal

10. Limiting factors—relative importance.

In general, to what degree do you think *personal factors related to yourself* may be limiting in implementing this guideline? (These factors might include poor relationships with staff, poor relationships with community people, lack of personal knowledge of community, and negative effects of insufficient skill.)

Rate the degree of facilitation:

None   0   1   2   3   4   Great Deal

In general, to what degree do you think *agency* factors may be limiting in implementing this guideline? (These factors might include unclear or shifting goals, programs, and/or assignments; lack of funds, facilities, and other resources; lack of support or hindering action of supervisor; and lack of support or hindering action of staff.)

Rate the degree of facilitation:

None   0   1   2   3   4   Great Deal

In general, to what degree do you think *client* factors
may be limiting in implementing this guideline? (These
factors might include negative response to organization
generally, clients interference with organization
activities, and dissensus among clients.)

Rate the degree of facilitation:

None   0   1   2   3   4   Great Deal

In general, to what degree do you think *community*
factors may be limiting in implementing this guideline?
(These factors might include negative response to
organization generally, lack of knowledge of
organization purposes, programs, or activities; influential
community groups or leaders that do not support
organization or program; and competition by other
activities with community residents' time and interests.)

Rate the degree of facilitation:

None   0   1   2   3   4   Great Deal

ILLUSTRATIONS OF INITIAL LOGS COMPLETED BY PRACTITIONERS

I. EXAMPLE OF PRACTIONER IN A WELFARE EMPLOYEES UNION

A. Goal Statement

Strengthen the union by developing its working class orientation and efforts through increasing the relative power of black and noncollege degree-holding members of the union. Shift organizational objectives from those of a traditional trade union to a greater working class orientation. Specifically, the proximate goal is to increase the effectiveness in performing union roles of members having a working class perspective. This will put into operation existing but dormant organizational goals.

B. Concretization (Operationalization) of Guideline Elements

Altering the structure of influence within the organization: Increase the relative (compared with white, middle class degree-holders) influence of progressive black and non-college degree members of the organization.

Increase the power of groups within the organization that have goals compatible with theirs: Through an educational program, increase the knowledge and competency of blacks and clericals; at the same time facilitate their movement into leadership positions.

II. EXAMPLE OF PRACTITIONER IN FAMILY SERVICE AGENCY

A. Goal Statement

Shift goals from serving clients one-to-one within the agency to serving categories of clients through outreach advocacy approaches. Specifically, the proximate goal is to have the board adopt a policy of advocacy for the mentally retarded population of the city.

B. Concretization (Operationalization) of Guideline Elements

Altering the power of influence within the organization:

Increase the influence of the Advisory Committee on Mental Retardation.

Increase the power of groups within the organization that have goals compatible with theirs: Helping the Advisory Committee on Mental Retardation to be active and competent in introducing pro-advocacy proposals into the board. The committee will be strengthened by making it more vocal, more unified, and more focused as a unit within the organization.

Notes

1. Meyer N. Zald, "Sociology and Community Organization Practice," in Meyer N. Zald, ed., *Organizing for Community Welfare* (Chicago: Quadrangel, 1967), pp. 33, 35.
2. Robert Morris and Robert H. Binstock, *Feasible Planning for Social Change* (New York: Columbia University Press, 1966), pp. 94, 102.

3. Edward Gross, "Universities as Organizations: A Research Approach,"
   American Sociological Review, 33 (4) (1968), 518-544; J. Gusfield,
   "The Problem of Generations in Organizational Structure," *Social
   Forces, 35* (4) (1957), 323-330; J. Mehina and C. Perrow, "The
   Reluctant Organizations and theAggressive Environment,"
   Administrative Science Quarterly, 10 (2) (1965), 229-257.

4. Edward Gross, "Universities as Organizations: A Research Approach,"
   American Sociological Review, 33 (4) (1968), 518-544.

5. J. Mehina and C. Perrow, "The Reluctant Organizations and the
   Aggressive Environment," *Administrative Science Quarterly, 10* (2)
   (1965), 229-257.

6. Talcott Parsons, "Suggestions for a Sociological Approach to a Theory
   of Organizations," *Administrative Science Quarterly, 1* (1965), 64.

7. Charles Perrow, "Organizational Goals," *International Encyclopedia of
   the Social Sciences* (New York: Free Press, 1968), Vol. 2 pp. 305-310.

8. M. Zald and P. Denton, "From Evangelism to General Service: The
   Transformation of the YMCA," *Administrative Science Quarterly, 8* (2)
   (1963), 216-234.

9. C. Perrow, "Organizational Prestige, Some Functions and
   Dysfunctions," *American Journal of Sociology, 66* (4) (1961), 335-341.

4

Fostering Participation

For many human service workers including planners, organizers, supervisors, and administrators, the subject of participation is central to their practice. Neighborhood and community development workers, including those in the early settlement house movement, have viewed grassroots participation as essential to their efforts.[1] Planners in institutions such as Community Welfare Councils and United Funds have long embraced "voluntarism," which in practice has meant the involvement of a cross-section of community "leaders" in policy formulation and program implementation. Social activists have viewed the mobilization of masses of people as an ideological imperative as well as a strategic necessity.

In the field of social work, participation has been viewed in various, but not always compatible, ways. In one view, participation is *a goal in its own right*. That is, in an impersonal urban environment where associational ties have been weakened and individual citizens feel impotent, the basic objective of community practice is the restoration of meaningful human involvement through participation.[2] Phrases such as "local initiative" and "maximum feasible participation" capture this meaning. Substantive results, such as specific health and welfare programs, are not as important in this perspective as the more fundamental objective of providing channels for ties among people or increasing their decision-making capacity. Participation, then, is an overriding objective.

In contrast, other people view participation not only as a means for achieving more concrete programmatic ends but also as a *constant, unvarying means*.[3] The arguments for this view are both philosophical and practical. In the first place, it is argued, democratic values require self-determination and the broadest possible involvement of the affected community in the development and enactment of policies and programs. Hence, maximizing participation represents a fundamental philosophical creed. In the second place, only those programs which are determined by citizens will be vigorously carried out; that is, when people take part in decisions affecting their lives, they will support the resulting public policies and programs. Thus, on a practical basis, participation is correlated with effective policy and program implementation.

A third view of participation is even more practical. In this view, participation is a *conditional means*, to be employed selectively for certain goals and under given circumstances. Not all valued social objectives, in this conception, will be achieved or maximized through broad participation. Some research studies, for example, suggest that raising the level of community involvement has had a negative impact on certain programs, such as school desegregation, school bond drives, and family planning. In this third orientation the practitioner would weigh the costs and benefits of participation in specific consequences to human welfare.

Regardless of which perspective one adopts, however, there follows the more pragmatic, "nuts and bolts" question of the best ways to get people to join, attend a meeting, work on a committee, or raise money for an organization. A school-community worker in an elementary school faced this kind of practical problem:

> The mothers program began in October and ultimately involved
> nine mothers—seven of whom did tutoring in the school with

youngsters needing extra help and two helping to maintain and operate the materials center. In April, the helping teacher who was in charge of the program came to me seeking assistance because two mothers had recently dropped out of the program and because she had only an average of three mothers attending their meetings.

We will focus our attention on this type of concrete practice task and set aside the philosophical ramifications of participation.

RESEARCH ON PARTICIPATION

Findings of recent research on the subject of participation can be summarized as follows:

The amount of participation in voluntary associations varies directly with both the number of benefits (rewards, satisfactions) offered by an organization and the degree to which the benefits are contingent on participation.[4]

Several studies suggest various refinements and elaborations of this proposition. Four points are particularly useful for our purposes:

(1) There appear to be four important sources of benefits that community-oriented voluntary associations can exchange for members' contributions: (a) achievement of specific goals; (b) rewarding goal-achievement procedures; (c) rewarding structural devices, such as formal offices; and (d) informal cliques.[5]

(2) Low-income persons show more interest in participating in activities that have direct and immediate benefits than in long-term activities with long-range payoffs.[6] Various studies of time orientation have shown that lower-class individuals have a greater present-time orientation, as compared with a future-time orientation, than middle-class people. (Some researchers have suggested that this

difference is caused by pressures on the low-income person to be preoccupied with immediate, recurrent daily problems of survival.)

(3) Low-income persons seem to prefer activities that provide opportunities for spontaneous, expressive behavior.[7]

(4) When benefits are explicitly tied to participation in a direct way, they have the greatest effect on participation. Warner and Hefferman, [8] for example, in a study of farmers' organizations, found that the greater the number of benefits that were contingent upon participation, the higher the attendance at association meetings.

ANOTHER ACTION GUIDELINE FOLLOWS;

PRACTITIONERS WISHING TO FOSTER PARTICIPATION IN ORGANIZATIONS, VOLUNTARY ASSOCIATIONS, OR TASK GROUPS SHOULD PROVIDE (OR INCREASE) APPROPRIATE BENEFITS.

The term *participation* in the guideline should be interpreted in a broad sense. It is meant to include not only the recruitment of new members but also changes in the pattern of existing members' participation. For example, an individual who had only attended general membership meetings might begin to participate in committee activities. We have not included the contingency notion in the guideline itself. It may not always be necessary or feasible, and some practitioners may find ethical dilemmas in making rewards explicitly contingent on participation.

ILLUSTRATING AND OPERATIONALIZING THE GUIDELINE

Of course, this guideline may be viewed as stating an obvious and well-known approach to fostering participation—that is, the provision of benefits to people to reward past participation and thus to motivate continued participation. Many practitioners intuitively use rewards linked to participation in this way. For example, Spergel, in a widely used community organization text book, states: "A service program tied in with community action assumes that there are persons who want to receive personal gratification as well as give energy and time to other people's problems. People expect a *quid pro quo*, one way or the other, for efforts expended."[9] What we are trying to do here is to make this common assumption and approach more explicit and more systematic, so that it may have a more effective impact on participation rates in community groups. We shall first describe the types of benefits related to participation and then demonstrate the use of each of these benefits through direct illustrations from practice.

Essentially one may describe rewards in terms of *instrumental* and *expressive* components. Instrumental benefits provide material, tangible, task-oriented returns (such as getting favorable legislation passed or a traffic light installed). Expressive benefits are intangible and psychological in character, such as increased friendships, personal satisfaction, and pride. (For some this may be reminiscent of task and socio-emotional aspects of group process.) Further distinctions may be made within the two categories:

(1) *Instrumental benefits* may be:

    (a) *material:* Obtaining an increased welfare allotment, getting needed information, or goods authorization

    (b) *interim-anticipatory:* Setting up an action structure or obtaining a verbal commitment that is a partial achievement leading up to the longer term material gain. (Indeed, these may also occur in steps together.)

(2) *Expressive benefits* may be:

(a) *social-interpersonal:* Making new friends or having an enjoyable social experience

(b) *symbolic:* Receiving an award that represents public approval or recognition of an individual's participatory activities, being mentioned in a newspaper article or newsletter

In practice these approaches may quite often be used in combination; sometimes one is given special emphasis and supplemented by others.

In the section that follows, practitioners describe how they used these four different forms of benefits with different client groups.

INSTRUMENTAL: MATERIAL

Our Community Mental Health program in the housing project was floundering. I decided to use the participation guideline out of a real need for it. I had been working with a small cluster of residents in the project to develop a self-help group. At one point, in the work with that group, our efforts began to falter, and we were threatened with losing the group, as a unit, although our consultations with individual families were going well. I decided to carry out this guideline with the goal of increasing participation in group meetings in that area of the project.

Following the elements of the guideline in this case really saved the group. We decided to increase benefits by making sure that specific personal problems were resolved for each family - for example, getting roach spray free from the manager (he usually charged residents) for two women; getting a toilet repaired; following through with the school in getting special attention for specific children; and transporting families to the dentist. At the same time we saw the families individually and informally and decreased the number of group meetings (where they had been weekly, we tried biweekly; then "on call"). In a certain sense, elimination of unnecessary meetings was a reward also.

When we felt that the time was right to call the group together, we did this and then personally visited those who did not attend, suggesting that we could not continue to work with them individually if they did not attend the group sessions. It absolutely worked— and the group was able to begin operating again. Thus by providing concrete benefits and at the same time making them contingent upon participation in the group, the group began to function again.

INSTRUMENTAL: INTERIM-ANTICIPATORY

I used this guideline to help in organizing the Black Student Union at the Junior High School. Although attempts had been made by the administrators of the school to organize the black students, lack of organizational skills had prevented the organization from functioning. After a meeting with the administrators, it was suggested that our Community Center give necessary assistance to organize such a group.

The assistant principal called a meeting of selected people to discuss organizational strategy. This step created some personality conflicts among students who were selected. Nonetheless, in that meeting I had the students identify the areas they felt the organization should concern itself with and had them divide into different committees. I assigned my staff to work as advisors to each committee, with me taking the Goals and Structure Committee. The Goals and Structure Committee, composed of about 10 students, met for five days to discuss the goals and objectives of the organization. Allowing the students to develop their ideas, and at the same

time influencing them to deal with concrete problems confronting
black students, the committee developed a structure that would be
composed of a Steering Committee with representation from each
grade level. I recommend that, as opposed to the traditional competitive election method, those students in each grade that were
interested volunteer and place their names in a box. The three names
selected from the box would be the persons on the Steering Committee. Other students would become members of the different
committees. Thus this method enabled students to be structured so
that their participation would provide some immediate resolution to
their problems. The Steering Committee began to function immediately, and staff again were assigned to provide technical assistance. The first step was for the organization to proceed with plans
for Black History Week. This effort enabled the organization to
immediately develop a program, carry it out, and allow for a large
number of black students to participate—thus providing the students with activities that gave concrete evidence of making progress
toward their goals, while gaining organizational experience.

After the black history program, the organization was functioning well enough, and had the necessary support and direction, that
I could withdraw my staff. Periodically, the students would call upon
us for assistance, but we had basically accomplished our task.

EXPRESSIVE: SOCIAL-INTERPERSONAL

Our union needed to increase the participation of the clerical members in our programs. A clerical caucus exists, but it is small, not
highly active, and has not engaged in any activity that has resulted
in the resolution of pressing problems or in satisfaction for members. Given the realities of our situation, it is not likely that there
will be any immediate resolution of these pressing problems, but
through sustained participation of clerical employees, along with
other groups, over a longer period such resolution is anticipated.
Nevertheless, to sustain the necessary participation it is important

that there be some short-term gratifications. The clerical caucus was encouraged to sponsor a social event which could raise money to finance legal support of our members and, equally as important, would bring more clericals together socially.

At a clerical caucus meeting in April, the decision was made to plan a cabaret night. Division of responsibilities for carrying out the decision was made. A day in late May was chosen for the event. During the remainder of April, the clerical caucus met regularly to plan the details of the party, choose the band, select the site, and distribute tickets to various union members to sell. People were obviously having fun and relating to each other differently from on the job or even in previous union business. My role was limited to securing from the union executive board the necessary advances in funds for deposits on the band and the hall and for the purchase and printing of the tickets.

The cabaret was a huge social success (although very little profit was realized). This led to an increased sense of camaradarie among those who had worked together on our event. Members of the caucus have a closer social bond among them now.

At a meeting in June there was a general feeling of job well done. Most of the meeting was spent recapitulating the events around the cabaret and, as we were about to adjourn, the decision was made to hold another meeting the following week and to begin to deal programmatically with the needs of the clerical employees, including how to recruit more into the union.

EXPRESSIVE: SYMBOLIC

As a school-community agent I was interested in increasing community participation in the school and at the same time improving services to children through use of volunteers. Special classes were decided upon according to the interests of the volunteers and students alike. They included arts and crafts, cooking, crochet, dramatics, modern dance, and sewing.

I decided to use this guideline in relation to the project in order to give continuity to the program. The "expressive" approach I took was to provide recognition for the work done by volunteers. This included: working toward a final presentation of activity "products" at the end of the program; giving service awards and pictures and publicity for the program. I kept the time short so that the end point would not seem too distant. I attended also to providing sufficient supplies; including the volunteers themselves in planning; holding frequent staff meetings to offer encouragement; and individual letters and phone contacts with volunteers. Much interest was developed in the volunteer program and it ran quite smoothly.

The continued staff meetings with the volunteers—and having the final event with publicity and service awards to look forward to—sustained interest in the program. The school administrator also took pictures and brought supplies during the six-week session. Weekly plans were required from the volunteers so that I would know what specific activities were scheduled and what could be done for the final presentation.

I requested that a regular PTO meeting be devoted to the final presentation, in order to reach a large number of community people. There was a great deal of publicity for the event in the neighborhood, as well as a picture and story in the *State Chronicle*. Volunteers and parents helped to publicize the program by word of mouth, I was delighted to see 200 persons in attendance at the meeting.

Because of the success of the program, the volunteers wanted to repeat it for another six-week session, and students also looked forward to it.

It is not necessary to dwell on the operationalization of this guideline, since the "benefit" notion is clear and is widely employed in the field. For a quick summary, the four illustrations from practice are laid out in chart form (Figure 4.1) according to the three components of the guideline: increase participation, voluntary associations and task groups, and benefits.

Setting	Increased Participatiomn	Voluntary Association or Task Groups	Benefits
Community Mental Health Housing Project	Tenants attend meetings more regularly	Self-help Tenants Group	*Instrumental Material*-free roach spray: have management make apartment repairs such as fix toilets; getting the local school to give special attention to children of the family; transportation to the dentist; legal aid service pre-curred
Junior High School Community Center	Increase number of black student service on committees	Black Student Association	*Instrumental Interim-anticipatory*: successfully conducting a black history program
Trade Union	Maintain membership and attendance at meetings of clerical workers	Social Work Union	*Expressive Social-interpersonal*: carrying out a successful cabaret night social event
School-Community Agent Program	Prevent loss off of participation of vounteers in providing after-school activities	Volunteer Service Program	*Expressive Symbolic*: a public PTO meeting featuring publicity, service awards, pictures, and display of products of volunteer services.

Figure 4.1: Elements of the Participation Guideline Operationalized

PERSPECTIVES FROM BEHAVIOR MODIFICATION

It is not surprising that a practitioner declared: "The guideline represents an application of 'behavior modification' theory to community practice - and this certainly seems appropriate." The benefits-reward (or reinforcement) principle is basic to behavior modification, and it would be a disservice to ignore the substantial research in this field as we apply some behaviorist concepts to community practice, an area in which they have not found systematic or direct expression. We have selected a few behaviorist terms and concepts that have a reasonable degree of relevance to community and organizational level intervention.

BEHAVIOR SPECIFICATION

It is essential that the practitioner specify the exact nature of the behavior to be changed. In the case of participation, we may attempt to increase the following:

(1) *rate:* the frequency with which an individual attends meetings

(2) *form:* the type or quality of participation - for example, attendance, committee chairmanship, financial or other material contributions, and speaking up more at meetings

(3) *duration:* the extent of participation - that is, retention or maintenance of participation over time

(4) *variability:* the stability or regularity of participation.

The assumption is that different types of benefits may be effective in encouraging various aspects of participation behavior.

POSITIVE REINFORCEMENT

Essentially this refers to the provision of benefits contingent upon the performance of some desired behavior. Thomas points out that the social worker has certain direct interpersonal reinforcers available in his relationship with clients.[10] These include approval, attention, and affection. In a group or community context, these rewards may be offered to a specific individual through other individuals. In classroom situations the following positive reinforcements have seen suggested: information regarding performance ("your answer is correct!"), material rewards (good grades, candy), social rewards (praise, affectionate embrace), and opportunity to engage in preferred behaviors (extra recess, personal selection of preferred study subjects).[11] In human service work the agency's resources offer many reinforcement possibilities, as do those external community resources with which the agency has operating linkages.

CONTRACTING

There has been increasing use of this concept in various settings, such as schools and community mental health programs. In our immediate area of interest it might be possible for a practitioner to come to an agreement about a level of participation, which if followed for a designated time might result in a pleasing outcome. For example, contracting was used in the issuance of a certificate to leaders who completed the six-week volunteer service session in the school-community example cited earlier.

SHAPING

This involves establishing a series of sequential goals leading up to a longer range goal. The technical behavioral language refers to "successive approximations." In community practice one is more likely to speak of *interim goals* or incrementalism. As a hypothetical example, a community worker wants a woman to take on an appointive office; she starts by asking her to attend a committee, then later asks her to chair a committee, and finally to hold an office.

GROUP CONTINGENCIES

Benefits may be offered to groups as well as to individuals. The United Fund offers a great number of social and symbolic rewards to volunteers who go over the goal, often using graphs and charts to dramatize the group objective. A committee or organization might set certain goals or standards for participation and foster group achievement satisfactions for successful attainment.

EXTINCTION

The extinction principle probably has a limited use in community practice generally. Here we are dealing not with rewarding a desired behavior, but with attempting to decrease undesirable behavior. This is riskier and more difficult, because it often evokes the use of punishing or aversive stimuli, usually by removing the reinforcing aspect of the interfering behavior.

For example, a member of the group persists in making very impractical suggestions, largely as a way of calling attention to himself. This throws the group off track and also causes the chairman to momentarily lose his control and effectiveness. The practitioner might suggest to the chairman that by responding in this overt way he is reinforcing this undesirable participation by giving special attention to it. Perhaps an alternative would be to ignore or to handle in a brief, routine manner these inappropriate comments and to proceed with the business at hand. The inappropriate participation thus might be extinguished when the psychologically desired rewards were no longer attached to it. At the same time, the chairman or the practitioner could respond with support and enthusiasm when the member makes appropriate and more practical suggestions.[12]

PATTERNS OF IMPLEMENTATION

In our review of the experience with this guideline, we found that one general pattern of implementation was followed. This pattern consisted of five steps: (1) goal determination, (2) selection of benefits to be used, (3) initial contact with potential participants, (4) followup contact with potential participants, and (5) delivery of benefits or operation of the event.

GOAL DETERMINATION

The first step was to select the participation objective. The guideline was used to form new groups or to maintain or increase participation in existing groups. Illustrations of these three objectives are given in goal statements of practitioners:

> My goal is to get those WRO (Welfare Rights Organization) groups in the metropolitan area which are not working to have the Early Preventive Screening, Diagnosis, and Treatment program implemented in their communities to participate actively in the efforts to secure this program for their communities.
>
> My goal is to maintain the current level of mothers now participating weekly in the mothers tutoring program in the school and to increase the number who attend the group meetings of the mothers.
>
> My goal is to increase the number of participants in the Mental Health Association's annual chapter leadership workshop.

SELECTION OF BENEFITS

The selection of the means of increasing participation may be seen as a two-stage process of identifying the benefits available or subject to the control of the practitioner and matching the benefits to the target population. One practitioner explicitly made this distinction when outlining her course of action:

(1) Figure out what might be the most effective reinforcers for this group.

(2) Figure out the most feasible reinforcers in terms of administration.

The order in which she lists the two stages is illuminating, since it suggests that practitioners may start by defining the benefits needed to increase participation and then attempt to obtain them, or first determine the types of benefits available and feasible in their situation. There is some support for giving early attention to the feasibility factor in the case of a practitioner who settled upon a benefit before verifying that it was, in fact, available: "During the week following this staff meeting I found that it would be impossible for the agency to pay for a luncheon for any portion of the staff."

The main concern, thus, would seem to be matching the benefits to the target system. In the absence of strong evidence concerning what benefits apply to which clients and constituents, the use of *multiple rewards* seems a wise course.

DELIVERY OF BENEFITS OR OPERATION OF THE EVENT

The actual delivery of the promised benefits is particularly important when the event is one in a series that was expected to continue. In many cases practitioners develop contingency plans, so that if one benefit turns out not to be available, another can be substituted. If the benefits are social-interpersonal, a good deal of energy has to be expended during the event itself; other types of benefits, particularly material, require much effort prior to the event. In general, the less certainty about the benefit—meaning the less control the practitioner has over the delivery of the reward—the more effort the worker has to expend on benefit provision. Practitioners just have to work harder, using multiple and contingency approaches, when their capability for "delivering the goods" is limited.

PRACTITIONERS' VIEWS OF PROBLEMS AND PROSPECTS

A number of reasons are offered for the utility of the approach. Several people comment that it was helpful in analyzing and planning their work.

> Most of us intuitively provide benefits for our clients and the groups with which we work. This guideline and the chapter accompanying it help us to analyze a situation much more carefully, to see elements we might not have, and to act in a more planful manner.
>
> The guideline illustrates the range of reinforcements potentially available and provides rationales for selecting rewards according to type of program and clientele.

Others note its wide range of application;

> New workers to an agency after appropriate orientation can use the guideline to get some things started. Workers who have been in the field should find the guideline helpful in the event they have become bogged down with the routine. All could find it useful in various kinds of experimentation in bringing different groups of varied backgrounds together.

Particularly when working with low-income groups, practitioners must be able to provide some rewards to keep these persons as functioning members.

At the same time, practitioners encountered some difficulties and therefore make a variety of suggestions on implementation of the guideline.

First, they point out that the benefits selected must have real meaning or significance for the target group. One practitioner states: "you must be sure that the benefits are really viewed as worthy by the group members. Without this the whole thing would have failed." Another practitioner notes that the benefits must be *perceived* as important by participants, regardless of the objective reality of the matter. He also indicates that the benefits could be potential as well as actual: "I increased the members' awareness of services which potentially could be provided—even if these were in fact not provided." The practitioners' experience also lends support to a point made earlier in this chapter, that if benefits can be shown to be clearly tied to or contingent on participation, the impact of the guideline can be increased.

Several practitioners highlight the need for interim, short-range benefits as a way of maintaining motivation over longer periods of time. As one puts it: "Often I feel a long range goal is achievable, but the community group may not be able to have that goal in sight— or even agree with it at that stage of the game." Another stresses the significance of this concept in working with low-income citizens:

> Most often, because of existing power relationships in the society, low income persons do not have the clout to make gains quickly or to resolve pressing problems besetting them. This means that their participation must be sustained while they go through the struggle to resolve these problems. The structuring of participation so as to provide expressive experiences and immediate social gratification permits this. Those of us who are highly issue-oriented tend to forget or neglect that. We dare not!

Several practitioners warn that these interventions cannot be carried out in a mechanistic, ritualistic manner. The art of practice has to shape the "science" of any intervention strategy. This involves the practitioner's attitudes, interpersonal skills, sense of timing, and so on. As two of them advise us:

> There is a need to develop trust and a decent relationship with client groups. This takes time and demonstrated proof that you can deliver.
>
> There is the consideration of the personal qualities of members as well as the level of enthusiasm conveyed by the practitioners.

In addition to the comments made above, which are somewhat general, more specific observations are offered by individual practitioners.

GIVE YOURSELF ENOUGH TIME

> Actually, I found little difficulty in using this guideline. The only problem was self-imposed: a limited amount of time in which to develop the "benefits" to be offered workshop participants.
>
> I would caution, to be very clear on the use of the guideline, do not over or under burden staff or the clientele you are trying to reach by trying to solve the problem in one day.

EXPECT TO ENCOUNTER SOME ORGANIZATIONAL OBSTACLES

> The usual organizational system interferences intruded; too many complicated chains of communication hindered application of a simple idea.

CHOOSING AND DELIVERING BENEFITS CAN PRESENT PROBLEMS

Since what would function as instrumental and/or expressive rewards varies by individual and by situation, simply determining what the reward might be was problematic. Also, it was not within my power to make available or to assure all of the rewards which might have reinforced participation.

Guaranteeing the rewards was the most difficult aspect of this approach.

Sometimes people can let the benefits go to their heads. The chairman of the S.C. Relations Committee received the "benefit" of signing the temporary food service licence. She is very excitable. Twice she got mad over something and swore she was going to have her name taken off!

OFFER SOME REAL AND TANGIBLE BENEFITS

I think that a practitioner who gets into the bag of promising only expressive benefits without any instrumental rewards is fighting an uphill struggle. And instrumental benefits are not only for "lower class people."

USE LOTS OF FOLLOWUP, INCLUDING PERSONAL CONTACT

The phone conversations were interesting. They proved to be key to the success of this guideline. For through these personal contacts, we were not only able to elaborate on the content shared in our letter to them, but we were able to respond to the personal needs and concerns of those to whom we spoke.

DO NOT PUT ALL YOUR EGGS IN ONE BASKET

A caution for new practitioners: I have learned from experience that no approach, used in isolation, is successful. I use this approach regularly in practice. I know that I can hold the most successful event, with all possible rewards, and still not get the desired participation. That is why we follow up this approach with others to insure the involvement we desire.

As we have stated, the benefit concept is both simple and commonplace. The challenge in its systematic application is to find additional and more powerful incentives for participation, within contexts in which community practice typically takes place. The truly creative task is to search out benefits that are highly meaningful or relevant for client groups and at the same time, available through agency or community structures over which the practitioner has influence, direct or indirect. Perhaps the most important contribution of the guideline may be to turn the practitioner's attention in the direction of new and more potent benefits that can be offered to clientele or constituents.

GETTING STARTED

SCANNING YOUR PRACTICE SITUATION

Think of some voluntary association or task group with which you are working that has a participation problem or consider some aspect of your practice situation that would be improved through setting up a participatory voluntary association or task group.

SPECIFYING PARTICIPATION BEHAVIOR

Specify the nature of participation behavior that you will be dealing with and the direction in which you would like to change it. For example, will you be dealing with: recruitment (retention or maintenance), increasing the rate of participation) changing the form of participation (membership, committee participation, officership, contributions, volunteer work), or stabilizing or varying the pattern of participation.

DETERMINING APPROPRIATE BENEFITS

Try to select appropriate benefits that are both attractive to clients and available to you to deliver.

What types of benefits would be potent or efficacious in stimulating the desired participation in the particular client group? Include instrumental (material versus interim-anticipatory) and expressive (social-interpersonal versus symbolic). Consider multiple rewards. Get to know your client group. Observe them. Ask them about their likes. Ask other experienced professionals.

What types of benefits are available to you to use through such sources? For example: your personal relations with clients; agency resources and good will; agency linkages with external resources; and the client group itself.

SELECTING SPECIALIZED REINFORCEMENT TECHNIQUES (IF APPROPRIATE)

Consider utilizing some special reinforcement technique such as shaping, contracting, group contingency, and extinction. These should be drawn on only if they are applicable and can be readily seen as potentially efficacious in your practice situation. Do not let them get in your way.

PHASING IN— CONTACTING POTENTIAL PARTICIPANTS

Consider a way of making benefits known and available to the relevant target group.

IMPLEMENTATION—DELIVERING BENEFITS AND OPERATION OF THE EVENT

Carry out the guideline—do not forget follow up contact.

ASSESSING OUTCOME

Assess the change in participation behavior that has been brought about by specifying empirical indicators of goal attainment. Empirical indicators may include:

(1) change in specific number of persons at meetings

(2) change in specific percentage of general membership who attend meetings

(3) specific changes in number or percentage of dropouts from the organization

(4) increase or decrease in the number of individuals who declare their intention to run for elected office

(5) increase the number of individuals involved in activities considered important by the group

I N I T I A L   L O G   F O R M

As a further step toward getting started, we suggest that you put down your tentative thoughts regarding implementation of the guideline. The Initial Log is a tool for organizing your thinking in a systematic way. It is geared especially to helping you think about your goal, ways of operationalizing the guideline, the key individual and community groups to involve, and the facilitating and limiting factors in the situation (personal, agency, client, community). Following the Log Form you will find illustrations of key sections.

INITIAL LOG: A PRELIMINARY GUIDE
FOR ACTION

1. Date of Preparation of Guide for Action _____ .

2. In relation to using the guideline, what is your proximate goal (i.e., type of participation and the amount of it)? Be as specific and concrete as possible. The goal should be moderate and short-range in scope (something that can be accomplished in 5 to 12 weeks).

3. Describe the circumstances (conditions, events, assignments, requests, etc.) that led you to use this guideline to achieve the goal above.

4. Look back at the intervention guideline. How would you begin to define or concretize *each* element of the guideline in your immediate practice situation (i.e., how might you operationalize these components)?

   (a) What is your proximate participation goal?

      Indicate *current* level of participation: _____

Indicate *intended* level of participation: _____

_____

Within what time period: _____

_____

(b) What benefits will you offer?

Instrumental

Material:_____

Interim-anticipatory: _____

Expressive

Social-interpersonal: _____

Symbolic: _____

5. How will you deliver these benefits?

    (Are they available to you? Do you control their use? Can you obtain some measure of control? Have you contingency benefits available?)

6. List the *major* steps you anticipate going through in order to utilize this guideline. Describe specific behaviors in the order in which you expect they will occur.

    _____

    _____

    _____

    _____

    _____

7. What *key* community groups will you probably involve (if any)?

Group   Reason for Contact

_____   _____

_____   _____

_____   _____

_____   _____

_____   _____

8. What *key* individuals will you probably involve (if any)?

| | Title and/or | |
Individual(s)	Affiliation	Reason for Contact
_____	_____	_____
_____	_____	_____
_____	_____	_____
_____	_____	_____
_____	_____	_____

9. Facilitating and limiting factors in guideline implementation.

As an aid to implementation you should consider factors that will affect your progress. We have provided checklists of common *facilitating factors*, those that will assist you to carry out the guideline, and typical *limiting factors*, those that may inhibit your success. In the checklists we have included conditions that were frequently indicated by practitioners in the field study. Others may be important in your own situation, and space is provided for you to note these.

Personal Factors

Facilitating

- ☐ Good personal relationships with staff.
- ☐ Good personal relationships with clients.
- ☐ Personal commitment to the agency.
- ☐ Personal commitment to the program.
- ☐ Personal commitment to the guideline.
- ☐ Personal knowledge of the community.
- ☐ Personal knowledge of the programs.
- ☐ Personal knowledge of the relevant ideology (and theory)
- ☐ Personal gain (promotion, job title, etc.).
- ☐ Prior experience.
- ☐ Self-confidence.
- ☐ Other: _____

_____

Limiting

- ☐ Personal knowledge of clients.
- ☐ Personal position or role.
- ☐ Personal loss (demotion, job title, etc.).
- ☐ Impatience.
- ☐ Other: _____

_____

Agency Factors

Facilitating

☐ Affiliated organizational support or involvement.

☐ Board support or involvement.

☐ Administration support or involvement.

☐ Supervisor support or involvement.

☐ Supervisor disinterest.

☐ Practitioner assignments are consistent with effort.

☐ Physical facilities aid the effort.

☐ Other:

Limiting

☐ Unclear or shifting goals, programs, or assignments.

☐ Hindering structure of the organization

☐ Negative agency attituteds toward the clients or community.

☐ Practitioner-organization conflict.

☐ Lack of staff or training.

☐ Lack of funds, facilities, or other resources.

☐ Lack of support of supervisor.

☐ Lack of support of staff.

☐ Other: _____

_____

Client Factors

Facilitating

☐ Client disinterest or dissatisfaction with the agency or program, leading to a desire for change.

☐ Other: _____

_____

Limiting

☐ Client disinterest or dissatisfaction with the agency or its activities.

☐ Client specifically disinterested in your program.

☐ Client lack of knowledge about the organization, its purposes, programs, or activities.

☐ Clients interfere with organization activities.

☐ Pressure from clients.

☐ Dissension among clients.

☐ Other: _____

_____

Community Factors

Facilitating

☐ Community receptivity to your organization or program.

☐ Support of (influential) community groups for your organization or program.

☐ External influences making the community support your organization or program.

☐ Community support of the practitioner.

☐ Other: _____

_____

Limiting

☐ Community residents lack necessary knowledge or skills.

☐ Community residents interfere with organization activities.

☐ Other activities compete for the time and interest of residents.

☐ Community lacks funds needed to support your organization or program.

☐ Other: _____

_____

10. Facilitating factors—relative importance.

This should indicate your perceptions of facilitating factors in a general sense.

In general, to what degree do you think *personal factors related to yourself* may be facilitating in implementing this guideline? (These factors might include good relationships with staff, good relationships with community people, personal knowledge of community, and positive effects of skill.)

Rate the degree of facilitation:

None   —   —   —   —   —   Great Deal
        0   1   2   3   4

In general, to what degree do you think *agency* factors may be facilitating in implementing this guideline? (These factors might include administration support, supervisor support, staff support, and physical facilities aid effort.)

Rate the degree of facilitation:

None   —   —   —   —   —   Great Deal
        0   1   2   3   4

In general, to what degree do you think *client* factors may be facilitating in implementing this guideline? (These factors might include client participation in organization or program receptivity to organization of program, and client support of practitioner.)

Rate the degree of facilitation:

None   —   —   —   —   —   Great Deal
        0   1   2   3   4

In general, to what degree do you think *community* factors may be facilitating in implementing this guideline? (These factors might include community support of organization generally, influential and other community groups support organization or program, changes in community tend to support organization or program, and community support of practitioner.)

Rate the degree of facilitation:

None   0   1   2   3   4   Great Deal

11. Limiting factors—relative importance.

This should indicate your perception of limiting factors in a general sense.

In general, to what degree do you think *personal factors related to yourself* may be limiting in implementing this guideline? (These factors might include poor relationships with staff, poor relationships with community people, lack of personal knowledge of community, and negative effects of insufficient skill.)

Rate the degree of facilitation:

None   0   1   2   3   4   Great Deal

In general, to what degree do you think *agency* factors may be limiting in implementing this guideline? (These factors might include unclear or shifting goals, programs, and/or assignments; lack of funds, facilities, and other resources; lack of support or hindering action of supervisor; and lack of support or hindering action of staff.)

Rate the degree of facilitation:

—	—	—	—	—	
None	0	1	2	3	4	Great Deal

In general, to what degree do you think *client* factors may be limiting in implementing this guideline? (These factors might include negative response to organization generally, clients interference with organization activities, and dissensus among clients.)

Rate the degree of facilitation:

—	—	—	—	—	
None	0	1	2	3	4	Great Deal

In general, to what degree do you think *community* factors may be limiting in implementing this guideline? (These factors might include negative response to organization generally, lack of knowledge of organization purposes, programs, or activities; influential community groups or leaders that do not support organization or program; and competition by other activities with community residents' time and interests.)

Rate the degree of facilitation:

—	—	—	—	—	
None	0	1	2	3	4	Great Deal

ILLUSTRATIONS OF INITIAL LOGS COMPLETED BY PRACTITIONERS

I. EXAMPLE OF COMMUNITY MENTAL HEALTH PROGRAM IN PUBLIC HOUSING PROJECT (FAMILY AGENCY)

A. Goal Statement

My goal is to increase tenant participation in the group meetings we are holding on "Y" Court in the Public Housing Project from representatives from five families at biweekly meetings to 10 families.

B. Concretization (Operationalization) of Guideline Elements

Increase participation in organizations, voluntary associations, or task groups.

Increase tenant participation in the group meetings we are holding on "Y" Court in the Public Housing Project.

Should increase the number of benefits (instrumental, expressive, etc.) provided.

I will try to do this by making sure that specific personal problems of each family that attends are resolved—like getting faulty plumbing repaired, obtaining free roach spray, serving as an advocate for children having difficulty in the schools, etc.

II. EXAMPLE OF BLACK STUDENT UNION IN A JUNIOR HIGH SCHOOL (SETTLEMENT HOUSE)

A. Goal Statement

My goal is to set up a black student organization which will be responsive to the needs of black students and not be controlled by the school administration.

B. Concretization (Operationalization) of Guideline Elements

Increase participation in organizations, voluntary associations, or task groups.

Increase the number of black students serving on functional committees of the black student organization from monthly average attendance of 15 on all committees to average attendance of 25 on these committees.

Should increase the number of benefits (instrumental, expressive, etc.) provided.

I am going to try to do this by having a group of students—operating as a committee—carry out a successful Black History Week program. This should not only encourage participation in the student organization, but also increase participation in the operating committees of the organization.

Notes

1. For a historical overview of the subject, see Sidney Dillick, *Community Organization for Neighborhood Department—Past and Present* (New York: Women's Press and Morrow, 1953).
2. For a prototypical representation of this position, see William W. and Loureide J. Biddle, *The Community Development Process: The Rediscovery of Local Initiative* (New York: Holt, Rinehart and Winston, 1965).

3. Murray G. Ross, in his widely read book, advocates this view. He states: "Community organization as it has been described here requires the participation of the people of a community. For what is to be united in common action is people. And what is to be changed is to be changed by people." Murray G. Ross, *Community Organization: Theory, Principles and Practice* (New York: Harper and Row, 1967), pp 168-169.

4. Charles Lee Mulford and Gerald E. Klonglan, "The Significance of Attitudes for Formal Voluntary Organizations: A Synthesis of Existing Research and Theory," paper presented at a meeting of the American Sociological Association, Washington, DC (September 1970). Leonard Schneiderman, "Value Orientation Preferences of Chronic Relief Recipients," *Social Work, 9* (3) (July 1964), 13-18. Alvin Seals and Jiri Kolaja, "A Study of Negro Voluntary Organizations in Lexington, Kentucky," *Phylon, 25* (1) (Spring 1964), 27-31. Keith W. Warner and William Hefferman, "The Benefit-Participation Contingency in Voluntary Farm Organization," *Rural Sociology, 32* (2) (June 1967), 133-153.

5. Harold Weissman, "An Exploratory Study of a Neighborhood Council," Ph.D. dissertation, Columbia University, 1966.

6. Leonard Schneiderman, "Value Orientation Preferences of Chronic Relief Recipients," *Social Work, 9* (3 (July 1964), 13-18.

7. Anthony M. Orum, "Structural Sources of Negro Student Protest: Campus and Community," presented at a meeting of the American Sociological Association, San Francisco (September 1969). Schneiderman, *op. cit.*

8. Keith W. Warner and William Hefferman, "The Benefit-Participation Contingency in Voluntary Farm Organizations," *Rural Sociology, 32* (2) (June 1967), 133-153.

9. Irving A. Spergel, *Community Problem Solving: The Delinquency Example.* (Chicago: University of Chicago Press), 1969, p. 136.

10. Edwin Thomas and Esther Goodman, eds., *Socio-Behavioral Theory and Interpersonal Helping in Social Work* (Ann Arbor, MI: Campus Publishers, 1965).

11. Mary B. Harris, *Classroom Uses of Behavior Modification* (Columbus, OH: Charles E. Merrill, 1972).

12. Aversive tactics are used by certain social activists (i.e.., Alinsky) or agency personnel (i.e., supervisors) to eliminate or shift particular behavior patterns or modes of participation.

5

Increasing the Effectiveness of Role Performance

After working for a year as a housing planner for a regional planning council in a large metropolitan area, a young social worker became concerned because his influence on the important organizations that shaped regional housing policy was minimal. He decided to take on a new role in order to increase his effectiveness:

> I had been responsible for the housing program of the Regional Planning Council without much sense of personal accomplishment and without feeling that the agency had achieved an influential role in the region with regard to housing matters. The goal was to increase my effectiveness through being viewed as an expert in the housing field by key decision-making housing agencies such as HUD and the State Housing Development Authority. In this way these agencies might use my advice in planning to a greater degree. The problem was they didn't expect me to function that way nor did my supervisor.

Human service workers often find themselves caught up in a crossfire of differing expectations regarding their work roles. Their own assessment of desirable goals may vary from those of supervisors, board members, community leaders, public officials, and others. Within the agency system different constituencies may have different views of a particular practitioner's roles. For example, clients and administrators may differ on how agency services of various kinds should be delivered.

It is often necessary for practitioners to deal with these contending expectations if they are to make an impact in their work. Also, in establishing a new role, or consolidating an existing one, differing expectancies sometimes become sharpened and brought into contention. Therefore, effective performance of newly emerging roles may be enhanced by developing them in such a way as to prevent, avoid, or minimize conflict.

GUIDELINES FROM RESEARCH ON ROLE CONFLICT

Various studies detail the dimensions of role conflict experienced by practitioners in the field. Gilbert,[1] for example, points up the contrasting expectations placed on OEO Community Action Agency staff members by agency executives and neighborhood client groups. Indeed, it is suggested by Krause,[2] in a study of rehabilitation counselors, that conflict is structurally built into some professional roles by specific devices such as legal limitations in defining the job, workloads, and production and time pressures that make successful performance impossible.

The existing research on role conflict seems to indicate that the most effective solutions include neither entirely personalistic reactions nor restructuring of the entire role situation. Rather, a blending or balancing of expectancies within the existing role (or range of roles) appears to offer greatest potential. This suggests the following generalization:

Effective solution strategies for role conflict involve compromising competing expectancies. Role clarity and consensus among relevant actors facilitate effective role performance.[3]

A natural inference to be drawn from this research generalization is contained in the Action Guideline:

> Practitioners can increase their effectiveness by defining a relevant role (or role aspect) and clearly specifying this role or role aspect and fostering mutual agreement among relevant superordinates concerning it.

The value of role consensus and role compromise is supported by numerous studies. Some evidence suggests that clarity and agreement with regard to role definition may have an important bearing on practice outcomes. In an exploration of this issue,[4] 30 county extension directors and their 75 county extension agents were interviewed on several dimensions of the agents' role: for example, direction and coordination, extension relations, educational leadership, and personnel management. The degree of consensus between a director and his agents regarding role expectations was assessed. In addition, state personnel rated the various directors on efficiency in program development and implementation. County directors who were rated more effective had higher consensus on mutual role expectations with their county agents than did those rated less effective.

Additional studies lend further support to this position. Demerath[5] found that lack of role consensus between various program levels impeded birth control in India. Gross et al.[6] concluded that lack of clarity concerning new roles thwarted the adoption of innovative educational practices among teachers. Rosen[7] determined that caseworkers in a public welfare bureaucracy exhibited high conformity to behavioral expectations when there was a high degree of consensus between supervisors and the practitioners, regardless of the type of influence or compliance mechanism used to achieve a designated role performance. Lyons[8] found that greater role clarity was correlated with lower job tension, lower job turnover, and higher job satisfaction.

In a study of professional orientations of social workers, Billingsley[9] found that workers with balanced orientations were much more effective, at least according to ratings by their supervisors. A study conducted in a mental hospital[10] attempted to determine factors associated with resolving conflicts in the direction of either patient satisfaction or organizational-staff requirements. Workers who used compromise solutions were rated by fellow staff members on the wards as most effective.

Compromising differing expectations is obviously not the only possible solution to this problem. Under conditions of role conflict, other solution strategies that are typically employed are: (1) emphasizing only one set of role expectations, (2) withdrawing from role performance, (3) changing the role definition, and (4) using aggressive and symbolic adjustment patterns.[11] Let us briefly explore the research findings on these solutions.

(1) *selecting one role for emphasis* (In a study of a shelter house for alcoholics,[12] it was found that counselors were expected to play the disparate roles of manager, companion, and member of the client community— counselors were former alcoholics. The main solution strategy they used was to select one key role to emphasize.)

(2) *withdrawal from expected role behavior*

(3) *realistic action to change the role definition*

(4) *aggressive and symbolic adjustment patterns.*

The last three mechanisms were found in the Krause[13] study of rehabilitation counselors. Withdrawal implies non-involvement— an apathetic, withdrawn response. Realistic action to change the definition suggests a mature, problem-solving posture. However, in the Krause study the situation was structured in such a way as to restrict successful employment of the strategy. Aggressive and symbolic behavior represented an acting out of frustration and anxiety in personalistic terms. Such behavior is generally not task-productive, but it may help workers maintain emotional stability when they confront an unresolvable practice task.

OPERATIONALIZING THE GUIDELINE

An illustration of the operationalization of this guideline is provided by the experience of the housing planner in the regional planning council referred to at the beginning of the chapter. Here is his description of the steps he took to increase his (and his agency's) impact on housing developments in the area:

> Planning agencies within the region receiving funds from the Department of Housing and Urban Development were required to annually prepare a document entitled, by HUD, "Initial Housing Condition." The nature of this report was to be a description of the "state of housing" in each particular geographical area in which a planning agency was located. The specific perspective of the Housing Condition report was, however, not detailed by HUD. I was given the responsibility by the agency to prepare this report.
>
> Our deputy director was concerned about "shaping up" our housing program and gaining credibility with other organizations. I decided to work out a specific housing-oriented role with him.
>
> The question for me became, "What is my role in regard to this function and what type of task will result?" For a number of reasons, I decided early in my own mind that I wanted my role developed as a housing data-expert. (I could conceive of several other roles that I might assume in regard to the preparation of the report. I might have decided, for example, to concentrate less on data, and more on implementation strategies. Or I could have highlighted problems as experienced by low income people and

expressed by them, in their own words, in obtaining adequate housing. This would have been in contrast to a completely data-oriented report.) I wanted the task to be the production of an initial housing condition evaluation that would represent an analysis and interpretation of all the available data on housing in this part of the state; basically an estimate of the housing needs of the Region for the next 10-year period.

When I had decided what I preferred in regard to the role, I talked with our deputy director, since he had control over the internal program of the agency. He agreed to my proposal, and we further agreed that issues of strategy and policy could follow in a later report. The questions of housing data on the one hand, and housing implementation strategy on the other, would not be mixed into the initial housing condition report.

I spent virtually full-time in the next four weeks working on the report and gaining an understanding of housing data from sources such as the U.S. Census, the agency's own population projections, and other places. A reasonably high-quality report was produced. A meeting was held with a few Council staffers who had read the report. The group included the agency's director, deputy director, regional planner, and management information director. They were unanimous in their opinion that the report was the most substantial analysis of housing needs and use of housing-data that had been prepared in dealing with our section of the state.

In addition to this meeting, I also received comments from outside persons who had received copies of the report. Among them, a data analyst from the State Housing Development Authority and a noted private marketing consultant, gave their support for the report and indicated that they were planning to use parts of it.

I believe that the comments of these persons within and outside of the agency had the result of gaining more respect for my technical competence in the housing field, which I consider one criterion of increasing my effectiveness. I do not believe that this would have been possible, if my role had not been defined—allowing me to concentrate on data-analysis—and if I had not gained agreement for this role and task conduct by my relevant superordinate—the Deputy Director of the Planning Council.

In summary, this young planner recognized that he was not being as effective as he wanted to be; important decision-making organizations in the housing field were not taking him seriously. He decided they would take him more seriously if he demonstrated competence as an expert in housing data analysis. Housing agencies he was dealing with were formal governmental bureaucracies that tended to respect formally established bureaucratic roles. Having clarified his desired role for himself, he thereupon discussed it with his agency supervisor, won agreement to proceed accordingly, and went on to a rather successful achievement. Obtaining this agreement with the superordinate was crucial in this case, because it permitted the practitioner to define his virtually full-time job activities for a four-week period in a particular way.

Another way to analyze the guideline is to break it down into its component sections and to discuss each in turn:

PRACTITIONERS CAN INCREASE THEIR EFFECTIVENESS

The practitioner needs to determine for himself an area in which he wishes to improve or increase the impact of his performance. Effectiveness implies a projected service or policy outcome; it does not relate to technique or role performance alone. The enacting of the role is expected to lead to a desired further outcome. In the example above, effectiveness was also related to being viewed and used as a data expert by outside agencies, not just to the completion of data-analyzing tasks.

A school social worker established a role as a consultant to teachers on individualizing pupils. She describes the *outcomes* of performing this role as follows:

> Thus far we have met with two teachers emphasizing that they individualize their approach to children. The outcomes have been encouraging. I'll give an example.
>
> We are dealing with a girl who: (1) had a low level of emotional expression, (2) had low self-esteem, (3) needed a warm affectionate environment, (4) was socially isolated in a rural home setting.
>
> (a) With regard to helping with emotional expression, the teacher set up weekly drama sessions, on a small group basis. The small group arrangement would insure participation of the student, and would provide a less threatening group situation in which to try out her emotions.
>
> (b) With regard to self-esteem, we decided to capitalize on the girl's fondness for and skill in games. She was encouraged to develop a game of her own. The class played it, with much enjoyment. The teacher has the class play this game once a week.
>
> (c) With regard to warmth and acceptance, the girl is released once a week to tutor younger children in a class where there is a very outgoing expressive teacher who has been briefed on the girl's needs. Also, the younger children have responded with praise and affection to the help given them.
>
> (d) The teacher called the local Brownies troop requesting that they contact the mother with information and an offer of service for the girl. This was seen as a way of giving her more social contact in an isolated situation.

BY DEFINING A RELEVANT ROLE (OR ROLE ASPECT)

"Relevant" suggests a link between the area of effectiveness aimed for and a role instrumental to such enhanced productiveness. In the housing planning example, the successful carrying out of a data-analyzing role was connected to being viewed as a housing research expert. The term *role aspect* is used to suggest that the dimensions of the role may be appropriately wide in scope or rather narrow and modest. In the example, broader roles might have included planner, planning expert, or general research expert. A more narrow role aspect might have included data expert in public housing or expert in use of cost-benefit analysis in housing analysis. The school social worker confined her consultation to a given population (the teachers) and to a specific purpose (helping them individualize).

CLEARLY SPECIFYING THIS ROLE
OR ROLE ASPECT

"Clearly specifying" is used in juxtaposition to "defining." The latter may imply a rather broad conceptualization of the role; "clearly specifying" demands that the role be sharpened definitively. It means the narrower delineation of a broader role; that is, "expert" becomes clearly specified as "expert housing data analyst."

AND FOSTERING MUTUAL AGREEMENT

Agreement may take various forms: an informal verbal assent, a memorandum of understanding, a public announcement by both or one of the parties, or an official document. Any exchange from a glance or a handshake to a formal, legal paper or procedure may suffice for mutual agreement. In the housing example, there was verbal agreement in a conference between the practitioner and his immediate supervisor.

AMONG RELEVANT SUPERORDINATES CONCERNING IT

In formal bureaucratic organizations, superordinates will usually be immediate supervisors. In the kinds of human service agencies and indigenous voluntary associations and social change organizations in which community practitioners often operate, the definition of "relevant superordinate" may be much broader. "Relevant" connotes an individual with the authority, influence, or power to legitimate or facilitate the *particular* role or role aspect that the practitioner wishes to enact. This relevant superordinate may be the immediate supervisor, or it may be a supervisor or administrative person one two steps up the line in a larger organization. It may need to be the top executive. Alternatively, it might be the board chair, a board committee, or the whole board. Sometimes, in the fluid and political world of community practice, a relevant superordinate may be a community person who has great influence over decisions and operations of the agency—a wealthy contributor, an important neighborhood opinion leader, or the mayor or ward chair. Determining the key superordinate is a crucial component in carrying out this guideline. In the housing example the immediate supervisor was the relevant person. However, other possibilities were considered and discarded.

PATTERNS OF IMPLEMENTATION

Many patterns of implementation logically present themselves and were in fact manifested in the field test. It is possible to use superordinates within the agency (a supervisor) or outside it (a powerful political leader with influence on the organization). Within the organization one may work through the administrative hierarchy or the board structure. Consensus may be along a continuum from highly formal (a joint letter of agreement) to quite informal (a nod of the head).

The most useful way of viewing approaches to implementation is to describe the process leading up to and following agreement with the superordinate. From our experiences, four modes emerge:

(1) agreement → exercising the role

(2) environmental legitimation or support → agreement → exercising the role

(3) demonstrating the role → agreement → expanded exercise of the role

(4) agreement → demonstrating the role → and exercise of the role.

We will illustrate and discuss each of these in turn.

Agreement → Exercising the Role

Looking at the Regional Planning Council illustration, we saw that the practitioner proceeded as follows:

(1) determined an area in which to increase his effectiveness (being viewed as a housing expert by relevant decision-making agencies)

(2) determined and specified an appropriate role (data-analysis expert)

(3) chose a pertinent vehicle (the initial housing condition report)

(4) selected an appropriate superordinate (his immediate supervisor)

(5) spoke directly with the supervisor and explained the role

(6) gained the supervisor's agreement to his carrying out of this role (verbal consensus)

(7) exercised the role (prepared a data-based housing report)

(8) circulated this report to external organization (HUD, State Housing Authority)

(9) received approval from these agencies regarding the quality of the report.

This was a fairly common and direct way of proceeding, particularly in a situation without complications (opposition by any of the relevant actors or groups). One additional factor to consider is the degree to which the practitioner is able to pursue the role with existing skills and information. In several cases practitioners had to seek additional knowledge before undertaking the new role, such as policies of other agencies, insurance policy provisions, and agency service data.

LEGITIMATION OR SUPPORT → AGREEMENT → EXERCISING THE ROLE

A crucial factor in the pattern of implementation is the degree to which the relevant superordinate is initially sympathetic to the role the practitioner wishes to fulfill. When there is considerable compatibility of outlook, a simple straightforward discussion and verbal agreement will suffice. In other cases, some prior support or legitimation may be necessary. A practitioner who wished to establish a client-advocate role (for retarded children) in a traditional family service agency first needed to convince her executive director (the critical superordinate) that there was considerable support for such a professional function:

> In my case there was no written role description, only a very vague agreement between my agency and the Act 54 Community Mental Health Board. Because my agency is a family counseling type, the executive really saw that as the major aspect of my work with families having a retarded member. I felt that this approach would only be crisis oriented and accomplish little. Rather, I saw a more comprehensive role directed toward broader problem

solving on behalf of the mentally retarded citizens of our county, and set out to accomplish this in a variety of ways.

First, I attempted to point out (in writing) what "is" and what "should be," then listed the "should be's" in some priority order for action. This really wasn't too difficult to do, but took a lot of time because it was necessary to talk with the executive frequently; to support all statements with accurate facts; and to test out ideas on a number of other agency professionals involved with the retarded. It paid off in a number of ways, the most important of which was the successful completion of the guideline itself! In addition it accomplished the total acceptance of my role as a comprehensive one in planning for all manner of "rights" and services for retarded citizens.

Her pattern of implementation can be outlined as follows:

(1) obtained general support from relevant internal agency actors (casework supervisor, staff opinion leader, and general agency staff), while also talking informally with the agency director

(2) obtained support from relevant community groups, especially the Association for Retarded Children

(3) used this support in discussion with agency director to obtain his agreement

(4) demonstrated role to superordinate (in community education, public relations, socialization, and the like)

(5) formalized role in written report to executive

(6) further legitimated role by gaining support of Board Priorities Committee on report

(7) obtained additional formal institutionalization of role by notifying Act 54 Community Mental Health Executive (a substantial portion of her salary came from this source)

(8) obtained additional informal legitimation of role by illustrative discussion with general staff.

Here the worker, a skillful community organizer, gained support for the role both below and above the level of the superordinate, and although the executive director was virtually boxed in, the guideline was carried out in a congenial, professional aura rather than in an acrimonious fashion. Clearly the tone of implementation is influenced by the practitioner's posture toward the "agreement process."

In another instance the practitioner started by having a discussion with the board chair, with whom she had a personal informal relationship. With this agreement achieved she spoke to the executive director (who was the relevant superordinate). This encounter failed, whereupon she prevailed upon the board chair to serve as a surrogate for her in achieving the director's agreement to her role.

Sometimes external community support may be important in winning over a relevant superordinate. A practitioner in a model urban "Street Academy" program wished to develop a role as a militant organizer. When a crises incident occurred in the black community, the worker aided various community groups in articulating their demands. These groups then supported the worker's position regarding the new role.

DEMONSTRATION → AGREEMENT → EXPANDED EXERCISE OF THE ROLE

This approach may be advisable when the role is particularly complex, unusual in the agency setting, or unexpected because of tradition or the perceived qualifications of the practitioner. Demonstration of the role clarifies what is intended, shows it can be done, and proves competence. The family service worker who wanted to play a client-advocate role in part used this type of "modeling."

The function and importance of demonstration were expressed by a human relations worker in a school system who wanted to serve as a facilitator-resolver in instances of racial conflict:

> Along with a number of other school personnel, I was asked to go to a high school where serious fights were occurring. My participation in that situation was a kind of turning point. I acted as a mediator between students an staff, and between students and students. Actually demonstrating my competence during and after this very serious situation helped to establish my role as facilitator-resolver.
>
> What was most important in the legitimation of my role was the actual demonstration of skills visible to supervisor, clients, community, and peers.

One of the possible pitfalls is that the worker may demonstrate, but not follow up by obtaining, formal approval. A school-community agent performed a community-oriented role, as opposed to functioning mainly within the confines of the building. She felt constrained, however, from going beyond the limited display of her new activities:

> It seemed better to me not to challenge possible negative reactions by making an issue of it at this time. This proved true. However, it also means that we may have to cover similar ground again in the future.

When there is significant disagreement regarding the role, the practitioner has two options: biding one's time until an opportunity to move presents itself (this may mean abandoning the role) or carrying it out as above at a level of low public or organizational awareness—that is, in a "low profile" fashion. One caution with this kind of demonstration is that the practitioner may be viewed as insubordinate or defiant for developing a role without prior authorization. Or, the role may fail because of lack of backup support. One way of mitigating these problems is to select a role aspect initially small enough to avoid such consequences.

AGREEMENT → DEMONSTRATING THE ROLE → EXPANDED EXERCISE OF THE ROLE

Because of the complexity and dynamic character of the human service field, official approval of a role does not necessarily mean that it will be accepted by the people who may be involved or affected by it—for example, clients, colleagues, and external organizations. Very frequently the role has to be demonstrated before it can be effectively or widely carried out, even if prior authorization has been secured.

The narrative that follows depicts this process. It was written by the school social worker described earlier. Her principal confined her to work with problem children on a one-to-one basis. She used the guideline to attempt to establish herself as a consultant to the teaching staff with regard to individualizing behavior problems within the normal classroom setting:

> The principal and I have been continually at odds concerning my services at the school. He has repeatedly told me that the only things he wants me to do involve individual casework with children. Because of this limited role definition I explained that I would only be able to be at the school 1 1/2 days a week, spending a greater proportion of my time at other schools. Initially he agreed to that but later called the coordinator of my department expressing concern about the reduction in service and asking for a meeting between himself, me, the coordinator, and the school psychologist. It seemed to me that he might be willing to negotiate about my job responsibilities in order to gain more of my time at the school. This seemed a good time to specify my role and get agreement on it.
>
> At the meeting the principal and I spelled out what we each saw as relevant things for me to be involved in; my list included a pretty clear statement on consulting with teachers. The principal agreed with this generally, but no specifics were outlined. However, after the next faculty meeting he called me aside to say

that some teachers had been discussing the whole area of communications with students and that this might offer a lead into the new role I had talked to him about.

The next week he set up a meeting which included himself, the school psychologist, me, and a teacher, for the purpose of brainstorming solutions to problems she was having with youngsters in her class. The meeting went very well. This is a difficult teacher who does not readily accept suggestions and I could see that the principal was pleased to have the suggestions coming from all of us rather than just from him. After the meeting, I suggested we might try this again since it had proved so useful. He was agreeable and said that he would announce it at the next teachers' meeting—he would explain to the teachers that on certain children we would be having meetings from time to time. He wanted to do it this way so that the first few teachers we met with would not feel they had been singled out, but would know this was now a standard procedure. I was pleased to know that he would even consider calling it "standard procedure." During this discussion, we came up with the name, Educational Planning Committee, for the group.

Following these events her new role continued to expand as it was perceived with increased confidence by the principal and the teaching staff. Some of the specific outcomes attained were indicated earlier.

The demonstration may have functions in addition to showing the role and consolidating it. It may also serve the purpose of allowing the practitioner to test for the role, as well as gradually to build up increased proficiency.

PRACTITIONERS' VIEWS OF
PROBLEMS AND PROSPECTS

This guideline contains a number of elements, and it also seems to touch an extremely personal chord (a personal view of self and where one is going professionally). Typical comments include: "I found this guideline confusing," and "Thinking through the guideline and deciding how to use it was difficult for me because of my own haziness about my role." At the same time, there were also expressions of enthusiasm for the guideline's helpfulness in aiding the clarification of important aspects of role definition. For example, the school social worker who broke out of her confining assignment as a counselor to individual children said:

> I was really excited about this guideline because my role, for external and internal reasons, has been very cloudy. I am pleased with the direction this strategy has provided.

The major problems concerned the guideline's complexity and the fact that it cannot be applied under certain conditions. While one practitioner asserted that, "For me this guideline was relatively easy and presented no problems," most people reacted more in keeping with the practitioner who commented: "I would caution would-be users that application is not simple. Most situations have a mixture of values and orientations." Another expanded on the theme:

> There is a high degree of interpersonal involvement in any conflict resolution situation. Therefore implementation is more difficult that it seems. Theoretically, gaining understanding and support from a superordinate is sensible. In reality the whole situation was a complex web of interpersonal relationships, rivalries, power stuggles, and rip-offs.

Another worker warned, "Others may view your move as politically threatening to their status in the agency or system and act to sabotage the effort."

The fact is, of course, that role clarity and consensus are not always functional. Role ambiguity and role contention may contribute to workers' autonomy or creativity or allow the pursuit of multiple incompatible objectives. On the other hand. they may be a means of maintaining control by upper level personnel through keeping workers off balance. When such considerations can be set aside, and the issue presents itself in terms of rational, task-oriented role performance, where the interests and objectives of the practitioner and his superordinates are compatible, then the guideline seems most applicable.

Thus, if there are irreconcilable differences in outlook or interest, it would not be appropriate to use this guideline in its given form. A union organizer offers these cautions:

> This guideline is very tricky. The question you have to keep in mind is if I clearly specify my role and tasks, will I be able to foster mutual agreement among relevant superordinates concerning them? This question becomes key if there are fundamental political, ideological, or partisan disagreements held by superordinates. This approach to practice reflects these disagreements, and to specify roles and tasks of that practice may result in an organizational crisis rather than increasing my effectiveness. I am not saying that this guideline is not useful. What I am saying is that you first have to determine the level of disagreement among relevant superordinates if it exists. This may indicate that you must first engage in a preliminary intervention. Where there is sharp disagreement over the goal orientation, the use of this guideline could very well heighten tensions and intensify disagreements and actually reduce the effectiveness of the practitioner and the agency by forcing both to deal with the internal dynamics rather than the function of the agency. Gaining agreement of superordinates depends on the situation; it may be better to keep superordinates uncertain as to moves of the practitioners and of the organization.

Several other problems are indicated.

One, the concentration on professional role may evoke some very personal reactions: Who am I professionally? What kind of status or influence am I seeking in this agency? Where am I heading in my career? One practitioner puts it this way:

> One element that I think affected my working with this guideline was what we call "theme interference." This means that my own personal dissatisfaction with my lack of control and leverage regarding assigned tasks crept into my use of the guideline. Feelings about my future career goals and ambivalence about graduate school are examples of this. This was the most difficult guideline for me to deal with because of my internal confusion about directions I wanted to go in.

Two, there was an initial tendency for practitioners to think very broadly about roles and, thus, to set objectives that were unattainable or that took too long to achieve. More finite roles (and role aspects) are recommended:

> I had trouble with the scope of the guideline. I tried to think of my role and tasks in larger terms, like to institute a halfway house program, or to develop referral programs with unions. I did not think of smaller roles that might have been used. This will be important to get across in the manual.

Three, in addition to stimulating personal introspection, the guideline may call for a substantial outlay of personal energy, as well as time:

> The accomplishment of the guideline was not really difficult but did require a considerable amount of initiative on the part of the worker; much written work and much verbal effort with the executive.
>
> A caution: I undertook this guideline with bright hopes that I would have gained the respect for my role within a few weeks. I forgot about the fact that time is a key respect-building factor.

Four, several practitioners make it a point to emphasize that demonstrating the role in a delimited way is helpful.

> My situation was traditional, but it was supposedly moving in a totally new kind of area, and although the philosophy was there, the willingness to accept the new philosophy was not there. I had to proceed to establish that, demonstrate it, and get it legitimized, and therefore the guideline helped me to think through the kinds of things I should try to do.

Other comments include the observation that not only conflict but also agency policies and regulations can lock one into a particular role definition. "I found it difficult to shift to a social change orientation in my community work because agency specifications require that a certain number of staff hours be spent doing social adjustment tasks." Another interesting observation comes from a supervisor in the juvenile court who suggested using a mediator in situations of role conflict. This is an especially meaningful suggestion when clashing values exist (such as punitive vs. rehabilitative orientations toward offenders). Mediation can be a means of ensuring that neither side loses out altogether. Or it can preserve both sets of values intact in circumstances where both are desirable or there is uncertainty about which is more effective. Additional reactions gleaned from experience include:

> The guideline is especially helpful when starting a new position or job situation.
>
> This is a good guideline to start with because if may be difficult to carry out the others until basic roles are defined.
>
> Establishing a role as an expert was helpful as a beginning step and facilitated moving into other roles.

GETTING STARTED

In attempting to use this guideline for the first time you might follow a thought-action process roughly as shown below.

(1) Ask youself in what way or ways would you like to *improve your effectiveness*—for instance in serving some specific new client group, obtaining funding for a particular purpose, or having your suggestions accepted to a greater degree by the agency staff (or board).

(2) *Think of a role (or role aspect)* that is linked with attainment of this increased effectiveness (client advocate, fundraiser, a committee chair).

(3) *Specify this role* in more particular form (become a women's rights advocate, a funding proposal drafter, or a chair of the staff program planning committee).

(4) *Determine a relevant superordinate* for authorizing or facilitating the role (a community group, the agency executive, or a board committee). (Is there reasonable agreement or possibility of agreement concerning this role between you and the superordinate?)

(5) *Determine a procedure for reaching agreement with the superordinate:* direct discussion, obtaining prior intraor extraagency support, working through a surrogate, demonstrating the role in a limited way, and so on.

(6) *Decide upon the form for agreement* (formal-informal, verbal-written, or public-private, for example) and how you expect it to be manifested. (Determine whether further support or legitimation by other people is necessary to stabilize the role.)

(7) *Enact the role.* (This is, of course, a complex phase that is only noted here.)

(8) *Assess the degree to which exercising the role improved your effectiveness* as set down in 1. (Are you now serving a specific new client group? How many in number? Are you raising more grant monies and how much? Are your suggestions being accepted to a greater degree and do the staff minutes show it?)

I N I T I A L L O G F O R M

As a further step toward getting started, we suggest that you put down your tentative thoughts on the implementation of the guideline. The Initial Log Form is geared especially to helping you think about your goal, ways of operationalizing the guideline, the key individual and community groups to involve, and the facilitating and limiting factors in the situation (personal, agency, client, community). Following the Log Form you will find illustrations of key sections.

INITIAL LOG: A PRELIMINARY GUIDE FOR ACTION

1. Date of Preparation of Guide for Action _____.

2. In relation to using the guideline, what is your goal (some more effective practice outcome based on clarifying and gaining consensus on your role)? Be as specific and concrete as possible. Think in proximate terms and with regard to short-range prospects (something that can be accomplished in a five to 12 week period).

3. Describe the circumstances (conditions, events, assignments, requests, etc.) that led you to use this guideline to achieve the goal above.

4. Look back at the intervention guideline. How would you begin to define or concretize *each* element of the guideline in your immediate practice situation (i.e., how might you operationalize these components)? Keep in mind the proximate goal stated in part 2.

   (a) What role (or role aspect) do you intend to establish (that is linked to intended more effective practice outcomes)?

   (b) Can you further specify this role with clarity?

   (c) What will be the basis for agreement?

   (d) What relevant superordinates will you involve?

5. List the *major* steps you anticipate going through in order to utilize this guideline. Describe specific behaviors in the order in which you expect they will occur.

   _____

   _____

   _____

   _____

   _____

6. What *key* community groups will you probably involve (if any)?

Group	Reason for Contact
_____	_____
_____	_____
_____	_____
_____	_____
_____	_____

7. What *key* individuals will you probably involve (if any)?

Individual(s)	Title and/or Affiliation	Reason for Contact
_____	_____	_____
_____	_____	_____
_____	_____	_____
_____	_____	_____
_____	_____	_____

8. Facilitating and limiting factors in guideline implementation.

As an aid to implementation you should consider factors that will affect your progress. We have provided checklists of common *facilitating factors*, those that will assist you to carry out the guideline, and typical *limiting factors*, those that may inhibit your success. In the checklists we have included conditions that were frequently indicated by practitioners in the field study. Others may be important in your own situation, and space is provided for you to note these.

Personal Factors

Facilitating

☐ Good personal relationships with board/board members.

☐ Good personal relationship with administrator.

☐ Good personal relationships with non-staff professional peers or friends.

☐ Personal knowledge of the programs.

☐ Personal gain (promotion, job title, etc.).

☐ Professional "disinterest".

☐ Other: _____

_____

Limiting

☐ Poor personal relationships with community people.

☐ Personal position or role.

☐ Professional "disinterest".

☐ Fatigue.

☐ Lack of time.

☐ Other: _____

_____

Agency Factors

Facilitating

- ☐ Affiliated organizational support or involvement.
- ☐ Board support.
- ☐ Administration involvement.
- ☐ Supervisor support or involvement.
- ☐ Supervisor disinterest.
- ☐ Staff involvement.
- ☐ Practitioner assignments are consistent with effort.
- ☐ Physical facilities aid the effort.
- ☐ Other: _____

_____

Limiting

- ☐ Lack of power and/or authority of organization.
- ☐ Lack of support or hindering action of affiliated organizations
- ☐ Lack of support or hindering action of administration.
- ☐ Lack of support of staff.
- ☐ Other: _____

_____

Client Factors

Facilitating

- ☐ Client participation in organization or program (voluntary).
- ☐ Client interest in organization generally.
- ☐ Client interest in program specifically.
- ☐ Client disinterest or dissatisfaction with the agency or program, leading to a desire for change.
- ☐ Client support of practitioner.
- ☐ Other: _____

_____

Limiting

- ☐ Client lack of knowledge about the organization, its purpose, programs, or activities.
- ☐ Pressure from clients.
- ☐ Dissension among clients.
- ☐ Other: _____

_____

Community Factors

Facilitating

☐ Community support of organization generally.

☐ Support of (influential) community groups for your organization or program.

☐ Influential or other community groups involved with organization or program.

☐ External influences making the community support your organization or program.

☐ Community support of the practitioner.

☐ Other: _____

_____

Limiting

☐ Community residents lack other necessary knowledge or skills.

☐ Pressure from community residents.

☐ Community lacks funds needed to support your organization or program.

☐ Other: _____

_____

9. Facilitating factors—relative importance.

   In general, to what degree do you think *personal factors related to yourself* may be facilitating in implementing this guideline? (These factors might include good relationships with staff, good relationships with community people, personal knowledge of community, and positive effects of skill.)

   Rate the degree of facilitation:

   ___   ___   ___   ___   ___
   None   0   1   2   3   4   Great Deal

   In general, to what degree do you think *agency* factors may be facilitating in implementing this guideline? (These factors might include administration support, supervisor support, staff support, and physical facilities aid effort.)

   Rate the degree of facilitation:

   ___   ___   ___   ___   ___
   None   0   1   2   3   4   Great Deal

   In general, to what degree do you think *client* factors may be facilitating in implementing this guideline? (These factors might include client participation in organization or program, client receptivity to organization or program, and client support of practitioner.)

   Rate the degree of facilitation:

   ___   ___   ___   ___   ___
   None   0   1   2   3   4   Great Deal

In general, to what degree do you think *community* factors may be facilitating in implementing this guideline? (These factors might include community support of organization generally, influential and other community groups support organization or program, changes in community tend to support organization or program, and community support of practitioner.)

Rate the degree of facilitation:

None   0   1   2   3   4   Great Deal

10. Limiting factors—relative importance.

In general, to what degree do you think *personal factors related to yourself* may be limiting in implementing this guideline? (These factors might include poor relationships with staff, poor relationships with community people, lack of personal knowledge of community, and negative effects of insufficient skill.)

Rate the degree of facilitation:

None   0   1   2   3   4   Great Deal

In general, to what degree do you think *agency* factors may be limiting in implementing this guideline? (These factors might include unclear or shifting goals, programs, and/or assignments; lack of funds, facilities, and other resources; lack of support or hindering action of supervisor; and lack of support or hindering action of staff.)

Rate the degree of facilitation:

None   0   1   2   3   4   Great Deal

In general, to what degree do you think *client* factors
may be limiting in implementing this guideline? (These
factors might include negative response to organization
generally, clients interference with organization
activities, and dissension among clients.)

Rate the degree of facilitation:

None   0   1   2   3   4   Great Deal

In general, to what degree do you think *community*
factors may be limiting in implementing this guideline?
(These factors might include negative response to
organization generally, lack of knowledge of
organization purposes, programs, or activities; influential
community groups or leaders that do not support
organization or program; and competition with other
activities for community residents' time and interests.)

Rate the degree of facilitation:

None   0   1   2   3   4   Great Deal

ILLUSTRATIONS OF INITIAL LOGS COMPLETED BY PRACTITIONERS

I. EXAMPLE OF HOUSING DATA EXPERT IN THE REGIONAL PLANNING COUNCIL

A. Goal Statement

I want to increase my effectiveness by being viewed as a housing data expert by key decision-making housing agencies like the Department of Housing and Urban Development and the State Housing Development Authority. (This should benefit my agency by giving it more influence in the housing field generally.)

B. Concretization (Operationalization) of Guideline Elements

Increase their effectiveness: Being able to influence housing development agencies in the region with regard to their planning.

Establishing a relevant role or role aspect: Becoming an expert in the field of housing.

Clearly specifying this role or role aspect: Delineate my role as a housing data expert through preparing the "Condition of Housing" status report for the Council.

Fostering mutual agreement: Gain a verbal understanding about the validity of my doing a strongly data based "Condition of Housing" report.

Among relevant superordinates: Approach the Deputy Director of the Council (my superior, who could legitimize my role in preparing the report) on this.

II. EXAMPLE OF PLANNING-ADVOCATE ROLE FOR SERVICES TO THE RETARDED (FAMILY AGENCY)

A. Goal Statement

To help provide (through our agency and other organizations) more comprehensive services to the retarded. Specifically to set up a volunteer program that would initially service 100 retardates.

B. Concretization (Operationalization) of Guideline Elements

Increase their effectiveness: Be better able to stimulate and provide comprehensive services to the retarded. Initially set up a voluntary program.

Establishing a relevant role or role aspect: Develop a planning-advocacy role for services to the retarded.

Clearly specifying this role or role aspect: Writing out the details of the tasks and activities that might be associated with the planning-advocacy role.

Fostering mutual agreement: Obtain verbal approval.

Among relevant superordinates: The agency executive (although backup support was sought from others including the supervisor, peer staff, and board committee).

Notes

1. Neil Gilbert, "Clients or Constituents? A Case Study of Pittsburgh's War on Poverty," Ph.D. dissertation, University of Pittsburgh Graduate School of Social Work, 1968.

2. Elliott A. Krause, "Structured Strain in a Marginal Profession— Rehabilitation Counseling." *Health and Social Behavior, 6* (1) (Spring 1965), 55-62.

3. Bond L. Bible and Coy G. McNabby, "Role Consent and Administrative Effectiveness." *Rural Sociology, 31* (1) (March 1966), 5-14. Judith Cotes, "Conflict Resolution in the Mental Hospital," *Journal of Health and Social Behavior, 7* (2) (Summer 1966), 138-142. Neil Gilbert, "Neighborhood Coordinator: Advocate or Middleman?" *Social Science Review, 2* (43) (June 1969), 136-144.

4. Bible and McNabby, *op. cit.,* pp. 5-14.

5. Nicholas J. Demerath, "Can India Reduce Its Birth Rate? A Question of Modernization and Government Capacity," *Journal of Social Issues, 23* (4) (October 1961), 179-195.

6. Neal Gross, Joseph B. Giacquinta, and Marilyn Bernstein, "Complex Organizations: The Implementation of Major Organization Innovation," presented at the meeting of the American Sociological Association, Boston, Massachusetts, August 1968, pp. 1-27.

7. Aaron Rosen, "The Influence of Perceived Interpersonal Power and Consensus of Expectations on Conformity of Performance of Public Assistance Workers," Ph.D. dissertation, University of Michigan, School of Social Work, 1963.

8. Thomas F. Lyons, "Role Clarity, Need for Clarity, Satisfaction, and Withdrawal," *Organizational Behavior and Human Performance, 6* (January 1971), 99-110.

9. Andrew Billingsley, "Bureaucratic and Professional Orientation Patterns in Social Casework," *Social Service Review, 38* (4) (December 1964), 400-407.

10. Cotes, *op. cit.,* pp. 138-142.

11. Gilbert, *op. cit.,* Krause, *op. cit.,* pp. 55-62. Lyons, *op. cit.,* pp. 99-110.

12. Krause, *op. cit.,* pp. 55-62.

13. Krause, *op. cit.,* pp. 55-62.

6

Conclusion

In the previous chapters we discussed each guideline separately and in its own terms. Here we make general observations based on using them together.

SEQUENCING OF GUIDELINES

While it is possible to conceive of each guideline as a discrete strategy for dealing with a given problem, it is useful also to think of combinations of guidelines that act on multiple related problems or objectives. Many practitioners suggest that there are many ways in which guidelines can be used either sequentially or simultaneously. We will offer a few suggestive possibilities that should stimulate the reader to think of others.

Some practitioners find use of the innovation guideline to be an excellent precursor to the establishment of a new role. For example, a school social worker was interested in functioning as a consultant to classroom teachers to help them improve their handling of children with behavior problems within the classroom setting. It happened that a helping teacher asked this practitioner for assistance in setting up a volunteer tutor program as an innovation in her school. The practitioner gave advice using the partialization principle as a way of instituting the new program. With the consultation role thus demonstrated, the practitioner was able to branch out and, through clarification and consensus with the school administrator, begin to operate in the desired broader consultation role with classroom teachers.

A regional planner productively linked these two interventions in the reverse order. He initially established a new role as a data expert in the housing field. This role provided legitimation and a platform for developing an innovation in which he and his organization became agents for screening new housing applications forwarded to HUD by local municipalities.

Another practitioner indicates the utility of using three guidelines sequentially:

> After working with these guidelines during the last year I feel that three of them can be used in the following order: promoting an innovation, establishing a new role, changing an organization's goals. For example, if a practitioner is capable of implementing an innovation it may facilitate clarification of a role for that practitioner. Often new persons seeking legitimation of roles or ideas may gain that legitimation best by demonstrating their idea, then possibly being responsible for continuing and broadening it after it has been accepted. Carrying out the role in a practical way allows the practitioner both to clarify what is involved for himself as well as to show it in action to other people in the situation. Based on a newly legitimated role, and having already shown competency in setting up an innovative program, the practitioner may be in a good position to tackle the more difficult task of making changes in organizational goals. The acquisition of a new role may put the practitioner in a much better position to implement a shift in organizational goals, especially through the mobilization of a group within the organization, a group to which he or she gains access because of the new role.

As an alternative, one guideline may be executed *within*, and as an expediting substep in, the implementation of another guideline. Examples are found in the manual chapters. Recall the family service worker who wished to introduce outreach services in a public housing project. To institute the service in the demonstration court, the worker developed participation there through the benefits principle. After the service has been instituted in that court, the innovation spread to other parts of the housing project. The participation guideline had serviced the innovation guideline in a supportive way.

It is evident that there are a large variety of possibilities for utilizing these strategies sequentially or simultaneously. Viewed another way, when there is a substantial shift in the practice situation—because of the practitioner, the organization he works for, the client population, or the larger community—opportunities for further change are frequently generated. Several studies have shown, for example, that changes in organizations often follow a turnover in leadership and that new patterns of participation in a community may develop when there are abrupt shifts in the social situation.[1]

The progression in the development of change opportunities may well be geometric rather than arithmetic, in the sense that not only does each change itself create a situation that offers new opportunities for further changes but also the multiple reactions in the total environmental setting to that change process may also be a stimulant for other changes. Obviously, it is ordinarily impossible to exploit the maximum number of change potentials. However, it makes sense to pause and look carefully at the variety of avenues opened by a particular intervention.

All-too-often our tunnel vision inclines us to a predetermined long-term effort in a particular direction while other short-term change possibilities remain unexploited. For example, in the rush to include minority oppressed populations in the internal decision-making process of OEO community action programs, practitioners often missed their chance, once the residents were operating effectively on the required boards, to take advantage of that newly

gained competence to move residents systematically into participation in any one of several other political, economic, and social
organizations.

Just as these guidelines may be variously interconnected in
practice, so may they be articulated differentially in the process of
study. The most useful order is probably contingent on the availability of relevant practice situations in which to implement them, and
such situations may flow naturally and unpredictably as a conse-
quence of any given implementation episode. Practitioner interest
and motivation is another important factor that should determine
the order in which they are taken up.

SOME FINAL COMMENTS

Thus far our discussion has centered on specific strategies and
outcomes. Now we allow ourselves the luxury of engaging in a bit
of prognostication and general professional discussion. Because
both nationally, and to a considerable degree locally, political alien-
ation is high and political patterns in flux, it is important to try to
note some of the areas in which the strategies we have explored may
prove to be particularly useful in the years ahead. Community
mental health efforts will probably gain momentum and offer a
fruitful field for the kinds of change efforts in which these strategies may be applied. The reorganization of health care at the local
level, particularly through the emergence of Health Maintenance
Organizations, suggests similar opportunities for intervention. The
development of the social side of urban planning posits a variety of
areas for guideline use. Despite the failure of many highly touted
urban educational programs, we believe that new and innovative
efforts ranging from comprehensive preschool and day-care centers
to special college programs for parolees will give rise to heightened
opportunities for the use of this kind of community and organizational level strategic thinking. We also predict a more vigorous effort
to build an integrated and more just society for the poor, and those

who are oppressed because of their age, color, sex, sexual orientation, handicap, or religion. Intergroup relations has always proved a fruitful area for interventions of the type we have explored.

If human service professionals are to take a hand in local politics, and many leaders in the human services suggest that this is necessary, then many of these approaches could clearly support that effort. The development of an effectively participating electorate may in part depend on the use of these and similar change strategies.

This manual may be used for in-service training to enhance and update the skills of a range of practitioners. One agency staff was able to use the material as a vehicle for initiating some long-desired changes in both their in-service training program and their approach to outreach efforts in the community.

The strategies are potentially usable not only by individual practitioners but also by groups of practitioners who want to explore together the most effective ways of initiating changes. One staff group, for example, met on a team basis using the goal change guideline to plan an approach for modifying goals within their own youth development agency.

The procedures incorporated in the manual, particularly in the Getting Started section, represent a general scheme for systematic problem solving—the consideration of particular factors in analyzing practice situations and the laying out of a series of steps and procedures to follow in formulating a plan of action. Through the repeated use of the initial log this type of analytic methodology can become internalized and, subsequently, can be applied automatically or by relying only on informal notes.

With regard to the manual itself, at this point the center of action has shifted to our readers. The name of the game in this instance is use, change, and human development.

Our experience with many practitioners and many agencies suggests that this material can help to make the pursuit of humanistic goals more systematic, tangible, and effective, as well as accessible to evaluation. If our effort can be regarded as an invention, then it is an incremental step on which others will need to build; our offerings must not be regarded as a rigid set of final prescriptions. Not only should the material be subjected to review but we also hope that it will be revised in light of the practical experiences of a wide variety of practitioners. What does not work should be discarded. We look forward to being updated and corrected. We give a set of tools that must be operationalized with skill. There is no magic in the guidelines, and no source of strength that can be used without the thoughtful application of discerning and committed practitioners. And there is little value in the manual unless that happens.

Note

1. Richard O. Carlson, "Succession and Performance among School Superintendents," Administrative Science Quarterly, 6 (1961) 210-227; Donald R. Trow, "Membership Succession and Team Performance," Human Relations, 13 (1960), 259-268

Appendix

A Note on the Research Methodology Shaping the Book

The study on which this book is based was sponsored by the National Institute of Mental Health and based at the University of Michigan School of Social Work. The project began by focusing on several problem areas or "practice issues" facing community-based professionals in the human service fields. These included questions such as how to encourage participation in community programs or how to gain acceptance of innovative agency services and programs.

This led into a retrieval phase in which an extensive search was made of the social science literature to discover empirical research finding dealing with these subjects. The acquired pool of knowledge was assembled, evaluated, and organized in the form of generalizations based on consensus findings within the existing research. In the next step the generalizations were converted into prescriptive form constituting a series of application concepts (or action guidelines). The action guidelines were then brought out into real agency settings in order to be field tested for applicability by agency practitioners.

The field study was conducted through use of a field staff of 22 practitioner informant field researchers[1] who were employed in a range of human services in the southeast Michigan area. The practitioners comprised a purposive sample selected on the basis of such characteristics as being: (1) competent, (2) reliable, and (3) conceptually able.[2] The field staff served as a corps of "social engineers" who had the task of operationalizing general action principles in concrete and functional terms, thus specifying patterns of implementation, ranges of activity in operationalization, and circumstances surrounding implementation. The project, with its action-research design, falls most closely within the research and development school of study.[3] A practitioner staff with special qualifications was considered necessary to fulfill requisite functions. Since there was some attrition during the one-year duration of the main field study, the number of practitioners implementing any given guideline varied. The field staff implemented action guidelines in the context of their normal agency assignments. They recorded their ongoing activities on log forms, which included close-ended checklists, and items calling for narrative observations. Logs were of three types: (1) the initial logs, which was basically a planning tool; (2) periodic logs, which recorded ongoing activities and behavior on a biweekly basis; and (3) summary logs which were completed after an implementation had been concluded and which were retrospective and evaluative in character. Practitioners received an initial orientation and regular supervision and support throughout the field study. Unit coordinators and the central project staff were actively involved in an intensive process of training, monitoring, and quality control. Logs received in the project offices were thoroughly checked, treated for accuracy and completeness, and routed for machine-data processing, as well as qualitative analysis.

The logs covered four general categories: (1) key community groups contacted during implementation (i.e., public agencies, private agencies voluntary associations); (2) key individuals contacted (i.e., agency staff, staff of other agencies, clients); (3) facilitating factors (personal, organizational, client, and community) in implementation (i.e., personal commitment, support of agency staff, client and community interest); and (4) limiting factors (personal, organizational, client, and community) in implementation (i.e., lack of time, lack of goal clarity in the agency, lack of knowledge in the community). These latter factors can be defined as any influences that serve to aid or hinder the practitioner in successfully attaining intended goals.

Results of the field study were in both qualitative and quantitative terms. Qualitative data includes general patterns of implementation, problems encountered, and advice offered. These are taken from narrative and open-ended items of the lobs. The more quantitative findings are based on standard checklists in the logs that were filled out by practitioners, both during the course of carrying out a guideline and at the end. These findings include groups and individuals involved in implementation and facilitating and limiting factors. This book contains mainly qualitative results.

The rating instrument used to evaluate the implementation process (outcome) was a five-point continuum ranging from no to complete attainment, framed in wording specific to each guideline. These continuum points were assigned a numeric value, ranging from 1 (none) to 5 (complete), indicating the raters' judgment of the practitioner's success in implementation of a strategy. The rating continuum for each guideline is presented below.

Guideline Four: Innovation

Innovation carried out (or accepted) by none of proximate general target system	Innovation carried out (or accepted) by a few members of proximate general target system	Innovation carried out (or accepted) by about half of proximate general target system	Innovation carried out (or accepted) by most of proximate general target system	Innovation carried out (or accepted) by all of proximate general target system

Guideline One: Changing Organizational Goals

No change at all toward intended new organizational goals	Slight attainment of intended new organizational goals	Partial attainment of intended new organizational goals	Considerable attainment of intended new organizational goals	Complete attainment of intended new organizational

Guideline Two: Fostering Participation

| Dropoff or no increase in participation | Slight increase toward intended participation | Partial increase toward intended participation | Considerable increase toward intended participation | Complete attainment of intended participation |

Guideline Five: Role Performance

| Practitioner achieved none of intended increase in effectiveness | Practitioner slightly achieved intended increase in effectiveness | Practitioner partially achieved intended increase in effectiveness | Practitioner considerably achieved intended increase in effectiveness | Practitioner completely achieved intended increase in effectiveness |

The rating continuum is not intended to be an interval scale; the numeric values were assigned for convenience in dividing practitioners into broad categories. Successful practitioners for purposes of our profile of successful practice were judged as obtaining a level of "considerable" (4) or "complete" (5) goal attainment.

Three raters with varying backgrounds and relationships to the project were used in this process, and standardized procedures were employed. The interrater reliability by guideline was .98, .90, .98, and .73 respectively.

The presentation descriptively highlights general tendencies in our practitioner sample. For purposes of this manual, the findings of the field study are abbreviated. We have found that a fuller presentation interferes with the reader's ability to focus on the application thrust of the manual. Fuller treatment of methods and findings will be found in other places.[4]

Some qualifying remarks need to be made here about the data from the field study. First, these are aggregated data for all the practitioners who participated, viewed as a total group. This causes some important limitations and problems. There were quite different circumstances surrounding the interventions of different practitioners. Furthermore, the practitioners held different positions in their agencies: line workers, middle management supervisors, and administrative personnel. Some of these agencies were large, formal bureaucracies; some were small, informal associations. Certainly it can be assumed that the specifics of intervention have varied among these different types of settings and according to certain background characteristics of the practitioners themselves.

Second, our sample is relatively small, although it is as large as could be managed with limited resources in a complex field study.

What is offered is a composite, suggestive picture of performance for a varied sample of practitioners. (The sample was selected to optimize a wide range of existing categories of people and settings.) This overview provides a preliminary general frame of reference for describing and analyzing patterns of practice. We hope that other researchers will be encouraged to do more detailed investigations so that the specific practice approaches of different types of practitioners in different situations will be given sharper focus. In a study concerned with both research and the creation of practical tools and products an inevitable tension is present. We keenly felt this duality. We might have tried to write a book that would have equally interested both the practitioner and the social scientist. After some experimentation that course was abandoned. We are reminded of the comment of a colleague who discovered a great diversity of student ability and interest in his class. The solution he formulated was to aim for the middle. His lamentful evaluation of that route was that "nobody was there."

Our solution in this instance has been to gear this manual to a primarily practitioner audience and to prepare a separate technical report for social scientists and researchers. Just as researchers may find the manual lacking in important ways, and perhaps of limited interest professionally, so may most practitioners find the companion methodological volume of little interest and of less use. A balance has been sought through different publications for different relevant audiences (updated with 1990's utilizations).

Litwak and Meyer, sociologists who were our associates at the University of Michigan, have produced an analogous practitioner's manual. In their work they attempted to apply a set of sociological theories to the tasks of school community agents. Their observations concerning their own situation have also much relevance to ours. Litwak and Meyer also chose to emphasize intervention approaches that would be of practical utility to operators in the field. The manual, they say, "is intended primarily to offer guidelines to practitioners concerned with local school-community relations of educational institutions. Practical suggestions are offered, sometimes in prescriptive language, as proposals for action rather than as rules. . . . We hope the result will be the posing of significant hypotheses to be tried by practice and tested by research."[5] This expresses also the spirit underlying what has been attempted here.

Notes

1. George J. McCall and J.L. Simmons, *Issues in Participant Observation* (Reading, MA: Addison-Wesley, 1969).

2. Claire Selltis, Marie Jahoda, Morton Deutsch, and Stuart W. Cook, *Research Methods in Social Relations* (New York: Holt, Rinehart and Winston, 1959), pp. 520-521.

3. Richard E. Schutz, "The Nature of Educational Development," *Journal of Research and Development in Education* (Winter 1970), 39-64; National Academy of Sciences, "The Experimental Manpower Laboratory as an R&D Capability," National Research Council, Washington, DC (February 1974); Edward B. Roberts, *The Dynamics of Research and Development* (New York: Harper and Row, 1964).

4. Jack Rothman, Joseph G. Teresa, and John L. Erlich, *Developing Effective Strategies of Social Interaction: A Research and Development Methodology,* PB-272454 TR-1-RD, National Technical Information Service, Springfield, VA 1977; Jack Rothman, *Social R & D: Research and Development in the Human Services*, (Englewood Cliffs, NJ: Prentice-Hall, 1980).

5. Eugene Litwak and Henry J. Meyer, *School, Family and Neighborhood: The Theory and Practice of School-Community Relations* (New York: Columbia University Press, 1974), pp. vii-viii.